Never Out of His Sight

I loved reading Cheryl's manuscript—she writes with such candor and wit! Knowing her over 3 decades, I was intrigued by the background story and thought processes of her journey through Judaism to Christianity; so many interesting life events. Cheryl has embraced a lifelong pursuit to know Jesus intimately and to walk in growing obedience to His Word. I'm confident God will use her story in people's lives as they recognize similarities to their own journey with Jesus.

—Debbie Tucker
Beloved Wife of Senior Pastor
Grace Church, St. Louis, Missouri

My wife and I live and serve in Jerusalem among Jewish people, largely because of the influence of Cheryl and her husband, Neil. They were the first Jewish couple to fan the flame of our passion for God's chosen and treasured people, inviting us to their home to celebrate our first ever Shabbat meal.

Then, the powerful love of YHVH, G-D of Israel, totally transformed Cheryl and Neil. Carol and I were blessed to nurture them in Yeshua as Messiah. They cherish G-D's grace to them as Jewish believers, practice Shabbat and Jewish feasts, and reproduce the fruit of Ruach HaKodesh around the world.

Before my wife and I moved to the Holy Land in 2014, Neil and Cheryl drove many hours to our home to pray for us . . . until next year in Jerusalem! Cheryl's exemplary spirit and extraordinary testimony in this book will help transform you and others with whom you share her dynamic story of grace and shalom.

According to Romans 9, "Theirs is the adoption, the divine glory, the covenants, the Torah, the Temple worship, the promises, the patriarchs, and from them is traced the human ancestry of Yeshua Messiah, who is God over all, forever praised!" Receive the revelation and pass this on to people you love.

—Daniel Ketchum, PhD
Isaiah 40 Ministries
Jerusalem, Israel

Chapter one ended, and I sat vigorously scrolling to the next screen on my phone. Seven pages into *Never Out of His Sight,* I learned more about my mom's life than I had witnessed in my forty-one years. To know that my grandfather felt the same burden of being Jewish, generations of the same blood now thunder in my ears. Though the path chosen for me has been littered with difficulty, my mom's wisdom has always led me home. With this book, I believe many lives will be touched and healed.

—Amy Skid Woelfel
Masters of Educational Administration

Cheryl Skid is the most contagious person I know. Contagious? Yes. Because you can't come away from visiting her without becoming infected by her love, passion, and mission for the Lord Jesus Christ. She is overflowing with the power and love for the Lord.

She is constantly seeking the Lord's guidance by reading the Word. She is daily in prayer. She is always questioning, always doing, always keeping the Lord foremost and present in her daily life.

I met Cheryl in junior high school. She was one of my Jewish friends. Through the years I prayed for my Jewish friends to come to Jesus Christ as their Lord and Savior. Forty plus years later, imagine my joy finding Cheryl had accepted Jesus. I was ecstatic.

I urge you to read her book. Tag along with her on her journey. You will find she is just like you and me. Full of struggles. Full of doubts. Full of the pressure of life. Yet she has overcome and is still overcoming the obstacles in her life because of her faith and trust in the Lord.

—Gloria Allen Reed
Editor/Writer/Reporter

I stand in awe of the woman I have come to know and admire over the last twenty-five years. A woman so full of love, she can open anyone's heart. I also stand in awe of her gentle yet honest voice as both writer and teacher.

—Nancy Balloni
Teacher, Special Education and Early Childhood
Children's Hospital of Wisconsin Volunteer

Never Out of His Sight

Learning to Discern the Voices

Cheryl Samelson Skid

Never Out of His Sight: *Learning to Discern the Voices*

ISBN 978-1-938796-01-2
Library of Congress Control Number 2016934554

Edited by
Connie Rinehold and Marjorie Vawter

Cover Illustration by
Fraser Leonard

Graphic Design by
Candy Abbott

Published by
Fruitbearer Publishing, LLC
P.O. Box 777, Georgetown, DE 19947
302.856.6649 • FAX 302.856.7742 • www.fruitbearer.com • info@fruitbearer.com

All the stories in this book are true, but some names and places have been changed.

Printed in the United States of America

Dedication

To every woman who is hurting today, take courage and watch what the Lord is doing in the dark that He can proudly display in the light. Be strong, my sisters. There is a day ahead that will bring full circle all the pieces of the puzzle that are swirling around your heart. If you are reading this book, you are my friend. I never have too many friends. All the things that were meant to hurt me made me able to love one more. John 18:9 Jesus promised the Father He will never ever lose one! The responsibility and the promise are His to keep.

To My Children and Grandchildren

Oh! How I adore you! You are precious, sterling silver, the brightest gold. You light up my life. You are miracles of restoration. I love you.

To My Mother

The wisdom of the ages is in your heart and mouth. I thank God for you daily.

To My Father, Now in Heaven

Pop, I always knew that wherever I strayed you would always find me.

To My Brother, Jeff

What a blessing you have been not just to me, but also to my children. They consider Uncle Jeff the prototype of what the perfect uncle should be. And me? I can't get enough of you!

To Neil

I'm glad we stayed the journey. I was a selfish young woman who had everything. You led me through hardship so that I became a woman able to share in the pain of others with a sincerity of having been there. Because of you, I have become well-acquainted with the hem of Jesus' garments. Because of you, I am who I am. I love you so much.

Table of Contents

Acknowledgments

Erica Miller

Not only was she an eyewitness growing up in our home, but also she combed through my manuscript with a keen eye. She edited for syntax and typos and also made critical suggestions for changes. I took them all.

Linda Stewart

Her professionalism as a college instructor in writing and a former Director of Communications for Urban Strategies, her suggestions for referencing people of color in various decades helped me stay true to the time and place.

Connie Vader Rinehold

Content editor and mentor, she kept insisting that I dig deeper, telling more until the manuscript has become a tool with which Jesus Christ can confront the reader with such a reality that hearts will melt under His gaze.

Candy Abbott

My creative, godly publisher, settles for nothing but the best when it comes to her authors. Thank you, priceless friend.

Women with a Vision

Dear friends and sisters, we walked the journey together, you read my book slivers, and you read my life. You love me as I am.

Never Out of His Sight

For a man's ways are before the eyes of ADONI *and He observes all their paths* (Proverbs 5:21 TLV).

We are never out of His sight. Even when our own behavior sickens us, our Heavenly Father never stops loving us. All we have to do is change our vision—to look where He is looking. He sees our destiny. It is beautiful. The longing we feel is Him drawing us.

The Lord appeared to us in the past, saying, "I have loved you with an everlasting love; I have drawn you with unfailing kindness (Jeremiah 31:3 NIV).

Introduction

God was limitless in His pursuit of me. I didn't know He was watching, so I lived as if no one cared or noticed or kept score. Perhaps my writing causes you to stop and think; perhaps a memory emerges and you start seeing where the Lord has pursued you. It has been the writing process in life that enabled me to rise out of quicksand, catapult over obstacles, and pop out of the potholes in my own life. As you read, you may uncover some long forgotten trap you'll recognize that God sprang for you.

When I read, I often put a book down, think and consider, pick it up again, write all over the margins, highlight what grabbed me, get out my journal and write. I hope you do the same. Enjoy with me: travel through the times of your own life. Get out those pens and markers. What makes you see the hand of God in your own life? What makes you want to repent?

Father God, the wonderful Creator, lover of our souls, and planner of our destiny is gentle and sweet. We have to look for the footprints in our lives in order to see where He has been at work. There are fingerpointers in our lives, as well—cruel and blatant accusations and deceptions of the enemy of our souls. Satan, the hater of God and all that is good, sets out to separate us from God the moment we are placed in the womb. Both are included in my story—footprints and fingerpointers. Perhaps you will recognize some in the story of your life.

I don't remember a Bible ever being read in my childhood home, yet, Bible truths seem to have been left like crumbs by an invisible Hand that can only be seen by looking back.

My days were ordered by Scriptures I didn't even know. Psalm 37:23 says that the steps of a good man are ordered of the Lord. It was as if the Lord gave me credit in advance for the life I would live later. Perhaps He ordered my steps early so that they would lead to the destiny He had for me.

Chapter One
What Is a Jew?

My parents met near the end of World War II when my mother was a hostess in a restaurant in California. My father walked in, flashing huge dimples and sparkling eyes.

"What's your name, soldier?" she asked, smiling.

"Joe. My name is Joe."

"Well, waddya know, Joe?"

As adorable as Joe was, that is how gorgeous Mary was with her shining auburn hair, worn in the fashionable pompadour, red brightening her full lips. He was 5'3" and she was 4'11".

That was day one of the ten days of dating before my father asked my mother to marry him. They made arrangements for her to take the train to Texas where they would be married by a justice of the peace.

"Does it matter to you that I'm Jewish?" my dad asked.

"What's that?" she responded.

It would be years until she would be able to answer that. Some people never can. It's a centuries-old question. What is a Jew? Some say it is a race. Some say it is a religion. Some say it is a culture. There are Jews who claim to be atheists. In fact, I would say that Jews can believe in anything except Jesus and be fine within the Jewish community. Some would say that Jews are people who believe in one God but reject the Messiah who sets "believers" apart from the rest of the Jews. But there are many Jews who do embrace Jesus as Messiah. I am one of those. Jesus, Matthew, Mark, John, Paul, Peter were all Jews. But Joe was looking at his beautiful wife-to-be and knew something that all who have Jewish hearts agree upon: it is hard being a Jew.

Joe decided that the best thing to do to introduce his wife to Judaism was simply to immerse her in the Jewish people. With absolutely no hesitation Mary said that whatever Jew was, she was fine with it. She would shed her old skin and take on his. Mary, at not yet eighteen years old, left her old life of a Southern girl from a tiny town where she had never heard of a Jew, never mind met one, and became a member of a Jewish community where she would become one of its most active leaders.

Mary was saying to Joe, "Don't try to talk me out of this. Whatever Jewish is, I'm in. Your Jewish God is mine. I'm throwing everything I came with into the trash. I'm yours, and I'm His." Mary was true to her word and clung to Joe, Judaism, and Sinai Temple. She served on every committee, served as president of Sinai Temple Sisterhood, and made delicious traditional Jewish dishes.

Joe passed away in 2003 and is buried in the Jewish cemetery. Mary's plot waits beside his. Is it random that my mother embraced Judaism, so that I grew up in Sinai Temple? That became my life, a footprint on what would become my future.

Mary had recently moved to California from a small town in the South, and she had never met a Jew. She looked into the dimpled face of her future husband. The question of his faith meant nothing to her. Since she had no pre-knowledge of Judaism, had never known a Jew or ever heard them discussed, the words dissolved into the air. Had she known what a Jew was, would that have changed things? Would it have mattered had she known that her children would grow up in synagogue with a constant reminder of the Holocaust before them in the face of their rabbi who had, except for his wife and small daughter, lost his entire family in the ovens? Would it have mattered that her children would face anti-Semitism? Mary and Joe were lost in each other's love, and Judaism could wait.

My parents married in Texas and then moved to Michigan City, Indiana. My mother got pregnant quickly. One day, while she was walking, she saw a malformed child with black hair growing all into its face, and she recoiled. Her reaction was so intense that she wondered if some curse were attached to that baby that was somehow contagious.

The pregnancy progressed, and my mother became very ill developing double pneumonia.

"My wife is really sick," my father told the landlady. "I need to invite the rabbi to come pray for my wife."

"No dirty Jew is coming into this apartment."

My father comforted his wife the best he could, swallowing the rage that his rabbi was not allowed to enter, but saying no more to push the issue. Little did the landlady know she was already housing two Jews, my father and a future convert, his wife. My parents made plans to move out of that hate-filled apartment as soon as was possible after the baby was born. He said nothing to his wife about the issue, heartsick to subject her to a life of this kind of pain.

My mother's labor was long, intense, and excruciating. After thirty-six hours the doctor decided on a Caesarian section. Out I came. Long black hair growing down toward my face. Coming out of her drug-state, my mother, still ill from pneumonia and suffering from long labor, stared at that little face and thought about the baby she had seen. Holding her little one, she pushed the memory of the malformed child out of her mind. As with most things in Mary's life that would threaten to disturb her, she chose to smother the thought. If there was a curse on that other baby it would not attach itself to her own. Actually, my baby hair fell out that was toward the face, leaving a pink-cheeked baby girl with blue eyes and a shock of black hair on her head.

Mary and Joe moved with their infant into a tiny house on Washington Park Boulevard, a street known by everyone as Knob Hill, in an area that had been built particularly for returning servicemen. The whole neighborhood was built on a sand dune. A walk out the front door, down the steps to the road, and following on to the right would bring us, after a long walk on sand, to Lake Michigan.

Our backyard led to a steep hill. What a place to grow up. Children everywhere, rolling down the hill, walking with parents to the lake, going to the dunes, and swinging off a thick rope with the knot on the end—a rope we called Tarzan. Jump. Grab. Swing. Hop off. Roll down the sand.

We ran in packs on our hill and we were safe. On hot summer days, my mother would blow up the rubber pool, just big enough to hold four little girls wearing nothing but panties. I was confused the day my mother told me that it was time to wear a shirt. I could no longer go outside in my bare chest.

My mother loved playing with us, as one of the children, and would often tell us longingly of the parties and fun she missed by marrying and parenting so young. I tucked that information away. I would look at the photo on the wall of my mother and father—young, smooth, unlined faces smiling toward their future. I felt so bad thinking that Jeff and I had cut short the joy of our parents' youth as they picked up the burden of parenthood.

The older I became, with all the tumult of adolescence, the harder and longer I looked at those unlined faces. The comparison between those faces and the ones I saw in my home were glaring. Gone were the unlined brows and bright eyes. Instead, there were furrows in the brows and deadened concern in the eyes. Guilty. I was guilty of ruining the joy and peace of that beautiful woman smiling from the wall. If I had studied harder, been cleaner, looked prettier, had more friends, maybe she would be less aware of me because being aware of me was being disappointed. I don't know where that sense of my being the cause of my parents' sorrow came from. They never communicated that to Jeff or me, that we were problems or burdens.

We have to get to the end of the Bible to open the envelope and find out why all the difficulties, the pain, the estrangements, the separations. From day one of our birth, even from conception, the devil has accused day and night.

There's something terrifying to babies about thinking they're alone, abandoned. We have played peekaboo with toddlers. We hide our face and peek out. In that little lapse of time when mama's face is gone there is a look of hesitation, loss, fear, and then comes the blessed face and joy!

You're there!

Satan's trick is to make us always feel we are alone.

My mother enrolled me in Fran Doll Mross's dancing class—tap, toe, ballet, and acrobat. In all the stages of my life she seemed to desire to give me everything possible. I was so tiny that my shoes had to be special-ordered, size 3 1/3. In those days did mothers even order costumes? My mother made mine. Tulle, slippery satin, and those sequins.

My mother worked with her hands to fashion things for me as an act of her love. She was acting out Scripture: *She looks for wool and flax and works with her hands in delight* (Proverbs 31:13 NASB).

One costume I remember was the penguin costume. I was supposed to be last in the line of the penguins. The dance routine included holding hands with the penguin in front of us and behind us with our leg thrown over an adjoining arm. We were hunched over to form a sleek line of black and white penguins. During one dress rehearsal I got out of order and ended up in the middle. So there I was, short little leg and foot perilously dangling in midair as I hopped along. The audience roared and I was humiliated.

Fingerpointer

Whose fault was it that I, the tiniest girl in the dance line, got into the middle of the line by mistake and stood there, foot dangling, hopping along to keep up with the other scooting girls? It doesn't matter. The goal of the accuser is to shame and humiliate. Sometimes adults unknowingly become part of Satan's plan to destroy, shame, reject. The audience was laughing—not as if to say, "What

an idiotic child," but most likely to say, "Look at that cutie with her foot up in the air." But it had Satan's desired effect on me, and I was ashamed, embarrassed, and felt that I made my parents mad at me.

I would learn to use laughter as a tool urging me on to be funnier and to lighten moods when they got dark. But, at the time, I was embarrassed about my diminutive stature. In kindergarten I was 2'10". My tallest height was 4'8". Later, as a high school teacher in rough neighborhoods I would joke with large male teens when they acted as if they wanted to intimidate me. Humor. It surely is a gift. I have used it in ministry all over the world to ease the pain of the truth of the messages that I shared. I am able to see the humor in my own blunderings and use it to help others make light of their own. God really did spread lots of humor in the footprints of my life.

"Watch it. When you least expect it, I will press this button on my thigh and fly up an additional two feet!" (I actually got that phrase from my brother.) At first, my teenage students would stare, then wonder at the possibility, but inevitably they would throw their heads back and roar. But, as a small child—the tiniest of the tiny—I spent most of my time embarrassed, ashamed, and wanting to fade into the woodwork. The one person who tried to make me feel better was a British woman who lived up the street.

"Don't make fun of Cheryl. She's dainty."

Now, I could really get happy about *dainty*. Did anyone take us aside and help us deal with our issues, like shortness? No. It was not the era of talk-show therapy. Just make it through. I was short. My head was patted. Taller people would lean over and use my head as an arm rest. I was a joke. I never took myself seriously because no one else seemed to. Years later, I embarked on a huge project.

"I don't know why I'm even trying," I told a friend. "No one takes me seriously."

"I do," she said. The lie that I had believed all those years was dispelled the moment she spoke the truth.

My mother had left all her family in the South, and I never really saw them until my brother was about to be born. Nano took the train up to stay with me while my mother was in the hospital. I had images in my mind of the baby and me tap dancing together in the hall on the *whoosh* air vent. But instead, there he was, all tiny and red, in a blue blanket. Dancing was out of the picture. I was four years old when he was born and would be going to kindergarten that winter.

The school was in what we might call the "urban" area of town and the students were predominantly African American. Did I see that as odd? No. I saw that as school, and it seemed perfectly normal to me. There were no people of color in my own neighborhood. There were lots of people of color in school. So school was where there were brown children.

What a trial for parents in the way of transportation. I didn't know anyone who had two cars at the time, so mothers would bundle schoolchildren and babies, drop their husbands at work, drive the children to school, retrieve them at lunchtime, bring them home for a homemade lunch, take them back to school, pick them up after school, and collect husbands from work. An alternative was to let children stay in school the full day and eat in the smelly cafeteria. I can still smell the room-temperature milk. But my mother chose to bring me home. I never felt that I was imposing. I always felt that my mother was doing what she wanted to do—take care of us, be with us, show us life in every way she could.

During the summer, my mother, Jeff, and I went to the beach almost every day. My mother and I would walk, and Jeffrey would be in the buggy. We grabbed big blankets, tossed them at the feet of my brother in the buggy, and headed down the hill to the beach. The sands of Lake Michigan are unlike any I've seen around the world. They are white and extend for miles. On really clear days we could see across the lake all the way to Chicago.

My father worked long hours, but occasionally he would surprise us. Spontaneously, he would say, "Let's go!" He would make a fire on the beach and cook for us or take us on a hike up Mount Baldy. Sometimes he would load us all into his pride and joy, his shiny black Oldsmobile, and take us for rides.

During some summers, Mother would take Jeffrey and me on the Panama Limited down South to see her family. I didn't know then what a luxury it was to have a sleeping car and to eat in the dining car. We would leave my father at home, spend a couple of weeks, and then he would drive down to pick us up. I remember the first time I realized that they were a couple and I was an outsider. My father got out of the car, and he and my mother ran into each other's arms.

I was so surprised. I'd never seen them be romantic. It was as if the world stopped spinning. If they were everything to each other, then where did it leave me? I never brought the subject up to them. It was too intimate. It was just one more piece of life that I was putting into the puzzle of who I was.

Chapter Two
I Can Be Different

Racial discrimination may have existed in Michigan City, but I didn't see it. Because my elementary school was predominately African American, dark-skinned people were just people to me. But something happened in the South on a visit that left an indelible print in my brain, one I do not want to erase because it helped to form the person I have become.

During a trip down South in the 1950s, I was with Janie, a girl from the neighborhood, and we were leaving the downtown area to go back to the house where we were staying. I scampered up the bus steps, calling back to Janie.

"Hey! Let's go sit in the back of the bus on the backseat!"

"No. That's where the n----s sit," my friend said, indignantly.

I stopped, dumbfounded, and looked at her. "They are as good as we are," were the only words I could form to show my horror.

"They may be as good as you, but they are not as good as me."

We rode back in silence. Once inside the house where my mother, Jeff, and I were staying, I ran to the bathroom and vomited. The sickness of that moment had struck me hard. I started to notice other things, as well. White and colored water fountains and bathrooms. Restaurants where African Americans couldn't go. Movie theaters where they had to sit in the balcony. My eyes were opened that day on the bus to notice what had been there all along.

I talked to my mother about it. After all, she was raised here.

"People think differently down here, but it doesn't mean we have to." She was her own person and so I, too, chose to accept that no matter how other people felt or believed, I could be different.

I would pull the covers over my head and whisper, "If no one can see me, am I really here?" Did anyone else ever do this? Or, elbows propped at the window looking out at the black, star-studded sky, "Is anyone anywhere in the world thinking about me right now?" I thought it was natural to feel invisible. My feelings were never probed. We were just expected to do our best and succeed in what we did. We weren't questioned about how we felt about things in the early years. Life in the 1950s was: enter a situation, try to figure out what was going on, and then fit in.

I do not recall a time during my life as a child or a teenager, even a young adult, when I knew of someone praying for me. No one said, "I'm praying for you." No one prayed aloud in my presence. But Jeff and I were taught to pray for others. I found a picture of us kneeling behind an ottoman in the house on Knob Hill. On the ottoman were four very distinct indentations where our elbows were placed as we knelt for nightly prayer. Our mother would lead us in "Now I Lay Me Down to Sleep" and encourage me to follow it up by praying for my brother, parents, aunts, uncles, and cousins. I would always end it with, "I pray for every little girl who has no one to pray for her tonight." Was that the seed of an intercessor?

My first lie and first spanking happened within minutes of each other. It was Easter morning, and I had gone out into the living room and found my Easter basket. Yes, we did the cultural Christian things that made kids happy. I took out a green sucker, tore off the tiniest piece of cellophane and licked it, then stuck it back in the basket. Later, I got spanked even though I insisted it was the Easter Bunny that had done it.

"It is true. He did it. I saw him do it! Why can't you believe me?" The spanking did not lead me to repentance. In fact, I don't believe I knowingly ever repented for anything in my childhood. But I had a deep heart-hurt for pain I caused my mother, even as a young child looking at the photos on the wall of that clear, unlined, fresh, hopeful face.

 Footprints 

The rod and reproof give wisdom but a child who gets his own way brings shame to his mother (Proverbs 29:15 NASB).

The Lord spanked me that day through the loving rod of my mother, but I didn't heed it. It would take decades before I stopped bringing shame to my mother. It is not enough to receive discipline. We must heed it. We must know it is right to obey.

Children, obey your parents in the Lord: for this is right (Ephesians 6:1 KJV).

Those were the days of doctors' house calls. One day, my mother called the doctor to please come and take a look at Jeff who had the measles. Dr. Bob—beloved by everyone—got to the bottom of the snowy, icy hill, and his car wouldn't make it. He parked and left it, then walked all the way up that slippery, steep hill with his black bag. He came in, good-naturedly smiling despite the schlep up the hill, took off his hat and coat, and handed them to my mother. He took a step toward my brother who was covered in spots, and stepped on what he thought was my toe. "Oh! Excuse me, Cheryl!"

But, I was on the other side of the room. Puzzled, Dr. Bob looked down, and instead of a foot, there was a squashed parakeet. I had let him out of the cage before Dr. Bob came, and therefore I was guilty of Petey's death. I don't recall anyone reprimanding me. But his death still rests on my shoulders. To make it worse, as I was preparing for the final writing of this manuscript my brother told me that the doctor felt so awful about killing Petey that he wouldn't charge for that slipping-sliding-torturous-hauling-up-the-hill house call.

 Fingerpointer 

No one blamed me. No one except the accuser who occasionally will hiss, Remember Petey the parakeet? You were the one who let him out of the cage you careless, foolish, unthinking girl.

Notice that he always talks to us at the age we were when he led us into the trap in the first place.

My mother was sad about Petey, but her immediate concern was that poor Dr. Bob had made that awful climb up a steep hill in an icy storm and then had to go back down. He was so nice. He would do anything for anyone. That hill was so steep. And to go down must have been even more slippery with nothing to hang onto for support.

That spring, the hill caused another problem. I had my tricycle at the top of the hill and somehow it slipped out of my hand and went all the way down the hill. My father asked me, "Cheryl was that by accident or on purpose?" I didn't know which word meant what, so I picked one. "On purpose." I don't remember my punishment, but I do remember that I must have chosen the wrong word—the first of several times that the wrong word got me in trouble.

I lied again that year. This time it was over a bowl that we were each to bring to class to use as a form for a *papier-mâché* gift. My mother sent me to school with a little fat round cereal bowl. Barbara's mother sent her to school with a large graceful salad bowl—the size to serve a whole family. Barbara painted hers a bright, happy red. I painted mine an ugly frog green. When the bowls were done I insisted that the red bowl was mine. I didn't get away with it. Of course, the teacher had been watching us day after day as we worked with our bowls so it was obvious that I was lying. My mother was called in about the bowls and confirmed that yes, my bowl was small and was not the large round lovely bowl I claimed was mine. I took home the ugly green bowl. I had the feeling that rather than being angry with me, my mother was sorry she hadn't given me a bigger, nicer bowl. I believe that my mother was so sorry for her early poverty that she determined I would have everything I needed to succeed, so if I didn't have it, I didn't get punished, but she herself took on the sorrow.

Chapter Three
Learning to Learn

I never fit in. It was as if there were a theme to life and I didn't know what it was, wherever it was, in any setting. In first grade we were given an assignment, and everyone got a failing grade for not following directions on where and how to print our names on the paper. I don't remember feeling particularly downhearted about it. Even then, it seemed silly to fail kids because they put their names in the wrong place. On the playground, a group of girls from our class stood together, crying.

"What's wrong?" I asked.

"Go away. We are crying because of our bad grade."

"I can cry with you."

"Go away! We don't want you in our little circle." I walked away. Why couldn't I cry with them? What was there about me that made me unwanted in the crying group? I saw a group of girls crying and wanted to join them in what they were doing. The bad grade meant nothing to me. That desire to fit into something not even remotely important to us can rob us of our true calling. I would have been more successful and true to my calling to go to the teacher to advocate for the girls—to ask her if putting the name on the wrong space on the page was really worth a failing grade. But I was too young to know that my calling wasn't—and never would be—to fit in but to lead up front and bring people alongside me.

Embarrassing memories emerge from my childhood years. On the playground a piece of equipment resembled a bicycle rack, but without the bars for bikes. We would lean toward it, fall forward holding on, flip over, and land on our feet. Well, I flipped over it, but my bottom landed in a mud puddle. So there I was sopping wet, wearing my little (things we remember) aqua nylon panties. I walked into the classroom.

"Well, just look at that. All wet." My teacher rumpled my wet backside then picked me up and plopped me on top of the radiator! Childhood is full of indignities which can lower our opinions of ourselves throughout the day. If that had happened to one of my children, I would be livid and be up at that school before the day was over.

But I never told my parents. Feeling embarrassed and undervalued was becoming normal for me. Was it because I was small that the teacher felt she could treat me like a puppet, just plopping me on top of the radiator with everyone watching? The same teacher asked me to go into the girls' bathroom and crawl under the stalls unlocking them all. Someone, as a joke, had locked them, and because I was small I was told to get on my hands and knees on the filthy floor where, no doubt, urine was splattered, and unlock the doors.

It was in the same bathroom that I had been left, forgotten, by the class and the teacher. I had been in the stall and everyone left. I was tall enough to open the stalls, but I was too short to reach the handle of the big door and had to wait until the next class came in. I was so scared in that big room alone.

Fingerpointer

You're locked in the bathroom. Aren't you scared? Everyone forgot about you? You will probably never get out.

I was terrified.

Just look at you on this filthy floor ruining your dress and getting icky stuff all over your knees and hands.

It never dawned on me to think how out of order that teacher was to ask a child to do something like that.

School. Is it a laboratory where unpleasant emotions form and mutate?

Nevertheless, I loved school. I loved books and writing and reading. I loved the students, the teachers, and the schedule. I remember feeling excited and happy when I heard my name come out of a teacher's mouth. I knew that when the teacher said my name something interesting was going to happen.

In Central School, Mrs. Swayzee taught me to read. She seemed ancient, dumpy with a white bun, stout legs, and sensible shoes. She sat us in front of a reading chart. I still remember the word *DO* and saying it like DOE and her saying, "No. It's doo." Those were the sight words. We also learned the schwa sounds—phonics. I don't know if everyone got it, but I did. We were placed in groups and, apparently, she believed in pairing the strong readers with the weaker ones, so I had to listen to the painfully halting reading of a male student.

After I became a teacher, I longed to teach children who fell through the cracks how to read. That desire stayed with me while I was teaching English and French, and later, Special Education. I finally found a program I loved and actually had the joy of teaching illiterate teens to read. That love of learning to read started in Mrs. Swayze's class.

Chapter Four
Does It Fit?

When I was eight years old and Jeff four, a nice house in the best neighborhood in which Jews were allowed to live became available. It was a huge move. We moved out of a tiny shoe box and into a lovely home with a fireplace on East Coolspring Avenue in Edgewood. I would leave Central School, which was probably 80 percent African American, to Edgewood School, which at that time had no children who were not Caucasians. There would now be three Jewish children in the school.

I said that it was the nicest neighborhood in which Jews were allowed to live because Long Beach had a charter, which *encouraged* homeowners not to sell to Jews or Negroes. To me the house in Edgewood was opulent. I remember thinking, "If I stand in the front yard, does someone drive by and think, *That must be a rich little girl*?" When we moved from Knob Hill to Edgewood, it was like moving from a back alley to Hollywood. I lay on my bed in my *own room* and looked to the other side of the room, and it seemed like it went on for yards. The bedroom was actually small, the furniture leaving little floor space, but that was the difference between the two homes.

How did we adjust to the change? When I started kindergarten at Central School I realized that my mother was sending me in a fresh dress every day, but other children wore their dresses for days in a row. So I had told my mother, "No. I need to wear this dress until it's dirty."

Then at Edgewood School, the children wore fresh clothes every day, so I did, too. I was, again, trying to fit in. Edgewood didn't have packs of kids, blown up swimming pools, or shirtless girls.

East Coolspring quickly became "home." There was a dining room where we ate together every night. The garage opened into an enclosed breezeway where we would watch TV in the summertime. In the colder months, Jeff and I played downstairs and watched TV on plaid couches. One morning, as we sat in the basement, something caught our attention. A *kitten*! A little gray striped kitten looked in at us from the window wells outside the narrow basement windows. We flew outside, tiptoed up to it, and petted it. He started to purr, and we were in love. We brought him to the door and called for our mother to come out.

"Can we? Can we keep him?"

"No! Absolutely not! Put it in the garage. Stray animals carry disease and fleas." But, once he was in the garage, he was *in*. In no time flat, he was living in the house, using a litter box, and ruling the roost. I loved Jinx. He was *my* cat. I told Jinx everything. All my problems, all my trials and victories. Jinx was my confidante. We were a perfect fit for each other.

Susan, a neighbor down the street, lived in a beautiful home furnished from a store that belonged to Susan's maternal grandparents. They had large expansive rooms and a big kitchen with a round table in the middle where Susan would eat her toasted bagel every morning. A winding staircase led past photo after photo of Susan at various ages. A formal dining room, a living room, a sitting room, Susan's bedroom—all beautifully appointed, but what took my breath away and drew me back time and time again were Susan's books.

My parents had books from a book club, boring adult books. Occasionally, my mother would pick up a Golden Book for me from the grocery store, and the public library was our home away from home. But Susan's books. They were huge bound books with gorgeous illustrations. The memory of the rows of beautiful books never left my mind.

I love books. To this day, I would rather shop for notebooks and books than clothing or furniture. Those books in Susan's library hooked me. I longed for something, but I didn't know what.

Eventually, I walked to school with Susan, but in the beginning I made the trek to Edgewood School myself. What causes a poor sense of direction? I've always had it. I'd close my eyes on my bed and when I opened them was always facing the direction opposite of what I had assumed. It was as if my inside compass was upside down and sideways. Nowadays, there are fancy names for it. Some people call it directional disability. Others coined geographical dyslexia. Whatever the name, it makes people feel helpless, and "less than," always having to ask for directions; then if the answer came "walk north" or "go south," they would get a blank stare. In dance class, I always had to pretend to close my fist around a pencil to remember which leg and arm were right.

When we lived on Knob Hill, it was too far to walk to school. Now, I walked. It was a simple walk from our driveway to Edgewood School. Go down the driveway and turn left. Turn right at the T and walk until I saw the school, which was on the left.

Every day for I don't know how long, I got lost coming home from school. Every afternoon, I set off from school and ended up totally confused. I would walk up to someone's house and knock on their door. All mothers were home in those days, so I would ask to use the phone to call my mother. While I waited for her and five-year-old Jeffrey to walk to get me, I would be tutted over, sat down, and comforted with hot chocolate and a cookie. My mother finally zoned in on my learning style. She drew a map for me with landmarks like, "wood pile" or "blue mailbox." That map in hand, with the picture of the woodpile and mailbox, was the security I needed. I never got lost coming home again. I got a firsthand glimpse of learning differences which proved so important in my life decades later as a teacher of students with disabilities.

Fingerpointer

This was intended by the enemy to be a finger pointed in my direction, his mocking voice saying, *See, you're the only one who can't find her way home. What a dummy! They had to tell you five times how to get to the school.*

Satan does all he can to destroy the confidence of God's children. When we can't find our way back to the car in a parking lot or remember which way we came out of a subdivision, we become dependent on people we can stop to ask—until that terrific invention, the GPS! But as He so often does, the Lord takes what the enemy meant for evil and turns it to good.

***The steps of a man are established by the* L*ORD*, *and He delights in his way* (Psalm 37:23 KJV).**

I loved school at Edgewood as much as I had loved Central School. Mrs. Kennington was my third grade teacher. I said that I never heard anyone praying for me my entire life until I was already a believer in Jesus. But she was remarkable in that she had Prayer Request Time every day. We prayed when families were in trouble, and when dads lost their jobs. I didn't feel a connection to God through the prayers, though. It was is if this was just one more thing added to the day, like "calendar" or "reading circle."

Mr. Wingert was my teacher for fifth and sixth grade, and he made me think outside of that elementary school classroom.

"One fourth of you will develop mental illness. Some of you will travel out of the United States."

He turned toward me then looked at the other students. "Just look at Cheryl. Her eyes are everywhere." I was pretty fidgety. Still am. But perhaps what he saw was not the fidgety, but the alert and ready. He also encouraged me to think beyond the life that seemed to have been given me. We are not stuck where we are. He broadened our horizons, but he did scare us about dangers of life.

"It's a jungle!" Mr. Wingert would say with a stance much like I later saw in Barney Fife of Mayberry. He would lean from the waist, stretch out his arm and declare details of wars, tragedies, atrocities of labor camps. But junior high! That was imminent, and it was scary thinking of going out of our little neighborhood where we all walked to school—all except for students who lived on farms—to a school that would take in students from every neighborhood in town.

Chapter Five
Grief

One day, Jinx didn't come home. It was not unusual for him to saunter off and come back three days later looking like Scarface. But this time . . . where was he? Then, one day, we found him. He had crawled into his garage. He came home to his family to die.

The pain. The agony. I cried over that cat with a deep grief, a pain unlike anything I had ever experienced.

We had a cleaning lady, Mary Norwood, who lived in an area in Michigan City called The Patch. The Patch was ramshackle with broken out boarded windows and crumbling walks. But, Mary knew Jesus. "Cheryl! Say this," she said. "The Lord giveth and the Lord taketh away; blessed be the name of the Lord." Sobbing, I repeated it after her several times as she held me against her large, soft, comforting brown body.

Footprints

How did I know that Mary knew Jesus? She obviously spent time with Him because her face shone. Moses's face shone because he spent time with the Lord.

It came about when Moses was coming down from Mount Sinai (and the two tablets of the testimony were in Moses' hand as he was coming down from the mountain), that Moses did not know that the skin of his face shone because of his speaking with Him (Exodus 34:29 NASB).

Shortly after Jinx died, we piled into the car to head down South for a visit. I loved those visits. The South was slow. Everyone spoke slowly, walked slowly. Life seemed to have been taken from the 78 rpm to the 33 rpm. S.L.O.W. Our first stop was to see Aunt Clara and Uncle T. J.

Oh, it was hot! Our black Oldsmobile was as hot inside as it was on the outside. No one I knew had air-conditioned cars. We drove 850 miles with all the windows open, hot air blasting faces and hair.

As we drove into the small town, we looked forward to getting out of the car and relaxing in our uncle's home. But something was wrong. As the car rolled up to the house, we saw T. J. standing alone in the doorway looking even smaller than his 5'1" self. We walked up and, instead of a big grin and rush to get to us, he just stood there.

"Didn't the state police catch you?" he asked. "Clara died today of a heart attack. We tried to get the police to let you know before you got here."

Beautiful Clara. Dead in her mid-thirties. She was gorgeous with black hair, cream-colored skin and a Bible in her hand. Even now I see her in front of a thin-paged Bible, reading and turning the pages. Her funeral was full of song, flowers, and people. The preacher gave a sermon about a sunset. My fresh grief for Jinx mingled with the sight of beautiful Aunt Clara lying in the coffin. It may seem awful to equate death of an aunt with the death of a pet, unless you have a pet. When I went back home, I wrote a poem about a sunset relating it to when God closes His eyes. I find that looking back on my early writings in junior high school they were reverent, of God. I was in His sight, even then; I just wasn't aware of Him yet. I had not yet tasted His closeness.

Summer was over, but instead of returning to Edgewood School, it was The Jungle, Elston Junior High. Nothing was the same after I left Edgewood School. In junior high, I was brought together with teenagers from all over Michigan City because there was only one public junior and senior high school to serve everyone, including the students who lived in Long Beach.

I loved to write. In seventh grade I began writing a novel about a girl growing up in the South.

"No, Cheryl," said Mrs. King, "you don't write about the South. You write about something you know."

I threw away my novel, assuming that because she was the teacher she knew best. I didn't bother telling her that my mother was from the South and we spent every summer in that slowed-down, polite, sultry, fried-chicken-dinners-in-the-middle-of-the-day land with Colored help in every home. I loved Mrs. King, and I didn't realize it at the time, but she could have discouraged me from writing. She made an assumption that I knew nothing about my subject, and I didn't have the confidence to stand up to her assessment. Teachers! They can encourage or discourage. They can show the way or block the door. I threw away the few pages of that novel, but I didn't stop writing, ever.

I began a love affair with words. I tried to increase my vocabulary by setting a goal to learn a certain number of new words per week. The thesaurus became my good friend. My English teachers knew I loved writing.

"Here, Cheryl. Enter this short story contest." I looked at the rules and deadline. I wanted it to sound really smart, so I made strong use of the thesaurus. I was writing about a teenage boy being zealous about a task he was doing. So, using the thesaurus I wrote: ". . . and with a flourish, Jack ejaculated as he finished the project." I imagine the judges got a good howl out of that one. I didn't win.

That misuse of vocabulary was bad enough, but then that summer . . .

"Mother, I am bored," I said dramatically, "bored of being boring, bored of being invisible, bored of being no one. Mother, I am so tired of being a virgin."

I got a long lecture on the advisability of using only those words with which I am very familiar and the meanings of which I am quite sure.

If the word "dork" was around in 1959, that would have been me. I was not attractive; I had braces, shapeless hair, and was self-conscious about my height. I always felt weird and creepy. I was sure that anything I didn't have or get was because I was too short.

I was trying out for cheerleading and went to every practice, but the day of the actual tryout I stayed home, sure I wouldn't make it because I was too short. I would rather eliminate myself than have others do it for me. There was another short girl, almost as short as I, who was actually popular. I didn't realize until later that my lack of "cool" wasn't in my height but in how I reacted to life.

Fingerpointer

There's that fingerpointer of ridicule again, trying to keep me from being in front of people because being in front of people was something to which the Lord was calling me all my life. The truth was, *You formed my inward parts; you knitted me together in my mother's womb. I praise you, for I am fearfully and wonderfully made. Wonderful are your works; my soul knows it very well* (Psalm 139:13–14 ESV).

For a time, I'd have quasi-fainting spells where I would just collapse. If I was in a classroom and the window was closed, I'd say I was claustrophobic and feel faint. These were not lies. I felt claustrophobic and light-headed and would fall down. For some reason, I got very nauseated before school and vomited almost every day. One day, I cut my hair off and just pinned it every which way. Odd. I was an odd duck in my school. My mother took me to the pediatrician about the fainting spells. This was the same wonderful doc that squashed Petey the parakeet during the house call.

"So you're claustrophobic."

"Yes."

He took me into a small dark closet, ushered me inside with him and shut the door.

"Now faint," he said. That ended that. Never happened again.

Chapter Six
Finding a Niche

Cliques formed. Where to fit in? There were popular, cute girls who had parties to which I was not invited. That made me feel sad until the stories came out about their drinking and passing out in the bathtub. Years later, that gave me a sliver-glimpse of the protection of God. Oh! How God protected me!

Footprints

Protection! How many of us looking back see the protection of God? Of course teenagers often think parents are just trying to keep them from any fun. It's a shame that we have to be this old in order to see His protecting hand.

But the Lord is faithful, who shall stablish you, and keep you from evil (2 Thessalonians 3:3 KJV).

We belonged to Sinai Temple, and I went to religious school from kindergarten through confirmation. The bud of the love of God started to emerge, just a tiny little sprout, but there, nonetheless. Activities at the Temple took precedence over activities at school, so Friday night basketball games took the backseat to Friday night services. Indiana was *the* basketball state, but my mother put her foot down. "It's Friday night. You'll be at temple."

In eighth and ninth grades, we had Mr. Goldman, a religious schoolteacher whose activities I really enjoyed. He opened our world, taking us to the People's Church in Chicago, to a Christian Science Church in Michigan City, and hosting interfaith activities. I started getting busy in the Jewish youth group. It no longer mattered that I wasn't invited to the Gentile girls' parties because the Jewish youth started becoming very cohesive and life, for me, was changing indeed. I began to sense the presence of God overwhelming me with the knowledge of Him, the desire to know Him, the longing to know Him, searching and searching and searching for Him.

I was in junior high and Jeff in third grade when we took a stand. We had a Christmas tree ever since I was born, even though my mother had left her Gentile background and fiercely embraced Judaism and the Jewish community. The Christmas tree was up as part of what America does in December, not to remember Jesus, because He was never mentioned in our home. But that December, Jeff and I made a decision.

"No more. We are Jewish. It's not right to have a Christmas tree in our house." We still continued to receive and give gifts at Christmas, and we had a special dinner, but that was the end of the Christmas trees in our house. (Actually many families hid Christmas trees in rooms not visible from outside, a fact I found out when mentioning this part of my book to Sinai classmates.)

The Jewish members of my Sunday school class remained a cohesive group until we were confirmed in tenth grade. We would go to Friday night service and afterward to various houses to have fun together.

Rabbi, himself, taught our confirmation class. We Jewish teenagers had been together now in Sunday school for ten years. We called it Sunday school because it took place on Sunday. On Sunday mornings our parents would drop us off at the Temple at 10:00, go home to enjoy the paper, coffee, and a bagel, and pick us up at noon.

Our religious training became more complex through the years. In elementary grades, we learned about the Bible heroes: Moses, Abraham, Daniel, Joseph. Then we transitioned into Jewish history: the history of the Jews in Europe, the history of the Jews in America. My favorite unit was a class where we learned basic Hebrew letters using a workbook where we were taught by a goat. On Friday nights Rabbi's sermons were on world events, particularly injustices. At that time, Jews found practicing their faith were severely punished by the hideous Communist regime in the USSR, so we had B'nai Mitzvah by proxy for Jews behind the iron curtain. When one of our group of boys turned 13 and made plans for his Bar Mitzvah, which included four years of Hebrew school and study with the rabbi, Sinai Temple would find a child in the Soviet Union who would study and celebrate his Bar Mitzvah the same day. There would be two chairs on the bema.

Rabbi Richter, our brilliant Rabbi, fluent in eight languages, had lost all his family except for his wife and daughter in the Nazi ovens. It influenced how he led us. Even as fairly young children, we would file into the community room, take seats on the floor, and watch films on the Holocaust: the ovens, the piles and piles of bony bodies, hair, teeth, shoes. So we would never forget.

Our scholarly Rabbi, who was honored throughout the nation for his teachings, had a look of sorrow in his eyes that never lessened, even atop his sweet smile. We were always very much aware that Jews were set apart—by themselves and by others. Instead of explaining our differences, it was just easier to hang around together. Rabbi Richter was preparing us to leave the familiarity of home as we all made plans for college. Part of his teaching our confirmation class was to arm us against the evangelists in college who would try to sway us to believe in Jesus.

"They will try to convince you that Jesus is the Messiah. You must understand this: the Messianic Age will take place when all hearts let go of hatred and turn to peace. When they insist, and they will, remember that there is no truth to what they will say—that Jesus was God's perfect son. He didn't even obey the Torah to marry and have children. They will try to make you believe in three—the Father, the Son, the Holy Spirit. There is one. Remember the Sh'ma."

In every Jewish service all over the world, a prayer was recited, *"Sh'ma Yisroel, Adonai Elohenu Adonai Echad."* Hear! Oh Israel, the Lord our God, the Lord is one.

As part of confirmation, we had to write a message to deliver to the congregation. After we were done and we'd gotten home, my mother said these words, "You did us proud." That was one of the few compliments I ever received from my mother, and those few words still feel so delicious in my heart today.

What I did that made them proud was the way I delivered the message. I don't remember a word of the message because Rabbi had read mine, found it lacking, and rewrote the entire message into something I would never have written or even thought. But, I was able to deliver it brilliantly. I felt inside of me that I was reaching everyone in the sanctuary with my words and my eyes.

How I got the nerve to try out for the school play I don't know. I was insecure and hated rejection. Yet, I auditioned and got the lead role as Miss Pinkerton in the play "Swingin' High." I not only got the role, but when my parents were outside waiting for me, they were swamped by people telling them that their daughter "has what it takes!"

Something happened during that season that taught me a fundamental lesson about God. There was a hayride to which dozens of teenagers were invited. I don't remember how it happened, but one student fell off the wagon and his leg was crushed beneath the weight of the wheel as it passed over him. I prayed fervently that Friday night at services:

"God, if you will heal my friend's leg, you don't have to answer my prayer to win for Best Actress." His leg was healed. I won best actress and was voted ninth grade most talented. I learned that God does not need our swap.

Theater showed me I could become who I was supposed to be. This was something I could tap into after I came into the knowledge of Christ, the mystery of Christ in me, the hope of glory. We don't have to be who we were. Were we liars? Unfaithful? Thieves? Murderers? We don't have to remain that even for one second. We can grab onto who we are in Christ. But that was many years down the road from Cheryl, the ninth grader at Elston Junior High School.

Chapter Seven

If Only I Could Believe That

Mr. Goldman, our religious schoolteacher, loved to take us on field trips. The one that held the most significance for me was the trip to Chicago to see the film *Ben Hur*. I watched a scene where Jesus interacted with someone. Jesus spoke so kindly, so graciously. His eyes melted into the eyes of the one to whom He spoke. The face looked back at Jesus with eyes that were big enough to hold the sky. I felt their rapturous joy.

Footprints

Jesus' breath was on my cheek. He was so close. In my memory of that scene I told everyone that Jesus was looking into the eyes of a woman. He looked at her with a face filled with love and her eyes seemed to absorb Him. Her eyes took in all of Him. Her eyes and His eyes became one pool.

My heart opened so huge that I wanted to swallow the truth. I was overwhelmed! Jesus! Jesus! But no. Jewish girls don't believe that. There was that accusing finger yet the "but" footprint was overcoming it.

Some friends challenged me as I was writing this book. "Cheryl, I don't think there was a scene with Jesus and a woman." I was sure there was. I rented the movie *Ben Hur* so I could find the place where Jesus was talking to a woman. There was none! That couldn't be right! I watched the entire film *again*. No scene of Jesus talking to a woman. The woman to whom Jesus was speaking in the movie was *me*.

I don't think I was even breathing during that scene. But Jesus wasn't for Jewish girls. Years before, my mother let down her guard and allowed me go to vacation Bible school with a young friend. I remember seeing flannel figures where the teacher was telling a story on a flannel board. She would pick up one person or animal and move it to help the story come alive to us as we sat and watched. I came home and started to sing "Jesus Loves Me." But my mother quickly shushed me and said, "Jewish girls don't sing that." Later, I was lying on my bed and reached up my hands, as I always did, to give Daddy God a hug goodnight.

"What if Jesus really *is* your son"—I shook my head—"Jewish girls don't believe that."

When I watched that scene in *Ben Hur* my heart longed, but I couldn't let it stay there. Many details of the film had faded, but not the feeling of longing as I watched Jesus and those eyes.

A couple weeks later, I went to Rabbi Richter. "When are we going to learn about God?"

"Cheryl, you are not ready to learn about God."

I felt abruptly dismissed. I drew in a breath as I stepped back. But part of me wondered if his great sorrow because of his family dying in the ovens made it difficult for him to present God to a girl of thirteen.

In ninth grade, some older girls enticed me with the possibility of riding around in their car during lunch hour. It was a thrill, but they were the wrong crowd. They smoked, wore lots of makeup, and weren't the type of girls with whom I was used to hanging around. My friends put their collective foot down.

"If you continue being her friend, you can't be ours."

It wasn't a "we are better than they are" prideful proclamation. It was a call back as from the Proverbs woman crying out to the vulnerable in the streets. I allowed them to pull me back to themselves, and I am not sorry, to this day.

In my junior year, I became friendly with a girl whose family life couldn't have been more different from mine. She and her mother lived in a small, sparse house at the edge of town. She had long black hair, wore flowered dresses and tights, and her mother had a haunted, Bohemian look. My friend was what we then called a beatnik but later would be called a hippy. I was a conscientious student who loved school, but at her insistence, I skipped one afternoon class and went with her to a local movie theater to see Tom Jones. In the lobby she started doing cartwheels all over the area. I didn't recognize "high" at the time, but she must have been. Thank God, He protected me from her stronger influence.

In high school, my interests narrowed to writing and public speaking. In English class, we wrote daily and edited each other's work. I majored in humor, sarcasm, and exaggeration. I loved making people laugh, even—and maybe especially—if it made me look bad. I was a natural in public speaking class and easily got As, so it was no surprise that my speech teacher wanted me to enter the speech contest.

I was usually a speaker who majored in "funny" but, for the contest, I decided to zone in on the subculture of my friend, the bohemian, who, in her desire to be different from all of us, was every bit the same as all the other long-haired, flower-skirted, black tights-wearing bohemians. Couldn't they see it?

My speech was called "Nonconformists: The Great Conformists." I received third place. In second place was a girl talking about her body in a mysterious way, about keeping our bodies pure because they were the "temples of the Holy Spirit." I had no idea what she was talking about. Teachers gathered around her to commend her for her courageous topic, but their comments didn't find a place to land in my mind. I had never read the New Testament or heard a sermon about the teachings of Paul.

But first place was something I could tuck away for later use. I had memorized my speech and presented it as a lecture. Not so the winner. He spoke in a casual, friendly manner as a neighbor would in the yard as he weeded the garden. The judges apparently loved his guy-next-door approach. First place.

Four years later, when I was out of the United States, my mother sent me an article from the local *News Dispatch*. The bohemian girl had died of an overdose. Prostitution supported the habit that killed her. If only I had known the Lord and had been able to introduce her to the One who is the ultimate Mood Lifter, whose overdoses are joy and freedom!

It came time for the selection and induction of new members to the National Honor Society. It was an enormous event. First, there was the scholastic requirement of being in the upper forth of the senior class. Next, votes were cast by the entire faculty and the current members of the school's National Honor Society. After the selection committee created the list of the new inductees, former members of the National Honor Society went through the city by twos after dinner, knocked on doors and standing at the door with a candle, presented the new member with a scroll. Was I flabbergasted when at 7:30 that evening there was a knock on my door. I was selected! What a shock. I felt neither brainy nor popular. I graduated as a member of the National Honor Society and Thespian Society having been given every possible tool by my precious and sacrificing parents to succeed.

Fingerpointer

You're a fraud. You don't belong to this elite group. It was a miscount. Or worse, they voted for you because they feel sorry for you. Maybe they think because you're not pretty you must be smart.

But God had plans for me! *"For I know the plans I have for you, declares the LORD, plans for welfare and not for evil, to give you a future and a hope" (Jeremiah 29:11 ESV).*

God knew what He had planned for me and chose for me the parents who would best direct me, the first part of the way, toward my calling.

Throughout my senior year, I continued to do theater and study piano. My mother wanted me to have every advantage that would make me well-rounded and able to fit into any social group. My father was interested in my character.

He believed in hardship for building character. If my mother tried to save me from a difficult situation, he was always quick to comment, "That builds character in her." And she'd reply, "Joe, if Cheryl gets any more character . . ." and never finished the sentence.

One of the most important skills my mother ever taught me was how to engage in conversation with people.

"Don't just stand there like a stick when someone walks toward you," my mother said after one of her acquaintances made a friendly overture toward me and was met with a blank stare and no body movement.

"Be warm. Extend yourself. Reach out and give a hug. Smile. Be friendly." It was a lesson I learned and have kept all these years, maybe even taking it over the top, judging by the rolled eyes and quickly retreating backs of my daughters when I approach strangers as if they were long-lost friends.

Chapter Eight
The Internal Battle

At the beginning of my senior year I found a diet in one of the popular women's magazines. I had always felt fat, although I don't think I really was. In fact, judging from old photos there was no excess of fat on me, but I felt fat, so I started the diet and stuck to it to a T. By the end of my senior year, I weighed 78 pounds. My family praised my commitment. Never did they express any concern that I was going too far. One of my best friends, Joanne, had a mother who didn't mind telling me the truth.

"You are losing too much weight."

I thought she was trying to sabotage my success. But her words were not sabotage; they were concern. Later, my college roommate told me that when she first saw me she thought I was sick, like with cancer, because I was so emaciated.

My mother was a wellspring of excellent advice: both timely and timeless. When I became an atheist in my senior year after reading *The Fountainhead* by Ayn Rand, I spewed my disbelief onto my thirteen-year-old brother. "Don't rob him of his faith unless you can give him something better," she said.

Footprints

What a horrible thing it is to shred the faith of someone else. I picked up Ayn Rand's book and, although I don't even remember the story line, I remember that it made the concept of God seem totally ridiculous and I spread that into the mind of my thirteen-year-old brother.

I don't know how they did it, but my parents instilled Scriptural truths in me without ever reading a verse out of the Bible in our home.

***"Whoever causes one of these little ones who believe in Me to sin, it would be better for him if a millstone were hung around his neck, and he were drowned in the depth of the sea"* (Matthew 18:6 NKJV).**

Another time, a friend was over and we were sitting by my brother. I made a joke at his expense in order to amuse my friend.

"Don't ever embarrass someone else in order to be funny." My mother was giving me the golden advice: never get a laugh out of someone else's pain.

I had a love for humor and a desire to make people laugh.

Despite my brains and popularity, my character was weak. I had lied, manipulated, and now, onto the scene comes a cesspool of sin to take me down farther.

The day before my graduation party, one of my best friends and I were in a store where her father worked. We went in to say hello and there *he* was. He was too old to be a boy. He was blond with blue eyes, and he was smiling at me. I don't know if it was my friend's or mine, but someone's mouth opened inviting this "man" to my graduation party. He swept me off my feet with his charm. I was seventeen. He was twenty-two and a Marine. He sent regrets with a bouquet of roses. Never had anyone sent me roses. I fell totally in love with this man. He took me out to expensive dinners several times a week and bought me lovely jewelry. Later, when I went to college, he sent me one dozen roses every week.

My parents sensed danger and denied permission for me to see him. He would stalk me, lurking outside my house in his car for hours. My parents were on panic alert. What could they do? Where could they hide me?

I was determined to be with him. My parents forbade it.

To my shame, I begged a lovely upstanding young man from the Jewish community to take me out so I could sneak off and be with the boyfriend.

"Cheryl, I respect your parents. I don't want to do anything to hurt them."

"Don't worry about it. I just have to see him and my parents will never find out."

He dropped me off to meet the Marine.

After my sneaky date, "Drop me off here," I told the boyfriend, "and I will just creep in the house. If they're up I will make up some story."

I walked in. Both parents were standing by the door.

"Where's your date?"

"Oh, he got drunk. His crazy driving scared me so I made him drop me off, and I walked." One more knife in my parents' heart. And it's too late to apologize to my Jewish friend. He died the year I began to write this book.

It would take shame to bring me to my knees—hurting my precious parents like I did.

That summer, before going off to college, I was working at my father's office as a receptionist. I was inept and rude and took advantage of being the boss's daughter.

"Cheryl, you need to be quieter out here. I'm conducting phone business."

"Close your door," I said dismissively, as if to a peer, or less.

"Cheryl, with those words you destroyed everything I have built."

I had eroded the respect people had for him and humiliated him.

My pop. Though my behavior in front of other people didn't show it, I loved my pop. It wasn't that he was so present in our lives. He worked a lot and worked late. He took classes and served on boards. But his presence was felt. It was so *there*. He was there in my heart all the time. I loved my pop. So why was I so rude and snippy? Maybe to show off as if to say, "This is what I can get away with because where he is your boss, he's *my* daddy and I'm the pride and joy of his heart."

Against that deplorable behavior toward my father was my sunshiny personality and friendliness with the employees. Two weeks before I left for college, they gave me a going away party, and the most memorable and useful gift was a turquoise umbrella. Would I need it in the frequent downpours! Indiana University's campus in Bloomington was huge, and we had to typically walk twenty minutes between each class.

One day, it came in the mail. My room assignment: Read Center, Clark Hall. And the name of my roommate: a girl named Sharon Pequenot from Pierceton, Indiana. I would be in a suite with a half bathroom separating us from the other two girls, whom I would find were named Janie and Jan, both from small towns in Indiana.

We packed the car, my parents got into the front seat, and I in the back uttering hateful phrases like, "I won't even miss you. I'll just miss my boyfriend." They knew my strong feelings for him but kept the ban on my seeing him or talking to him, which I broke without them knowing, time and time again. But who was sacrificing to send me to college? I was so ungrateful. So rebellious. Such a hideous heart. Sneaking out and lying to my parents had hardened my heart little by little until my behavior was almost unrecognizable from the girl I had been.

We drove the four hours down to Bloomington, parked in the oval entrance in front of Read Center/Clark Hall, and my parents helped me unpack the car and take my things to the third floor. They must have read how to survive dropping their college student off; it must have said to leave quickly to make the goodbyes easier. So we left my things in the room, took the elevator downstairs, and I said my goodbyes at the curb. I watched them leave, my mother not even bothering to wipe the tears that streamed down her face.

I had prepared by reading *Cosmopolitan*'s suggestions by Jake on how to make the best of the first year of college. The thing I remember was to get there early and get the best, top dresser drawers. I did. Greedy me, taking advice like that. Poor Sharon had to stoop down because I grabbed the top drawers.

Nothing prepared me for going away to college. During high school, some members of our journalism class had made a college trip to Valparaiso University, a little school—tiny, like a village compared to the enormity of a Big Ten university. Indiana University had 40,000 students on campus. Action was everywhere. Every night there was a party somewhere. Learning opportunities and influences—positive and negative—were everywhere. Negative: a fraternity house was right next door to our dorm and rumor had it that boys urinated on the carpets during parties. Positive: I got to see Peter, Paul, and Mary three times—free!

There were lectures several times a week. I loved lectures. I was able to attend many ballets and theatrical performances, but lectures were my favorite because I loved learning and cultivating new ideas.

Most of girls in my dorm were not interested in the arts or lectures. Some were farm girls who were brazen in telling me about their sexual exploits. They loved to play cards and roped me into playing Euchre for hours on end. But not Sharon. Sweet Sharon, a born again Christian, was stuck with me as a roommate. Despite my taunting her about her belief in this unseen Jesus, she never wavered in her faith.

Footprints

My roommate was from a Christian home, and her parents were so nice to me. Sharon tried to tell me about Jesus, but I ridiculed her so badly she really couldn't present Him very well. Yet, I remember so well how she spoke about forgiveness. She said that whatever we did, Jesus would forgive when we told Him we were sorry. I taunted her terribly about that, letting her know I felt that was like a "get out of jail free card." A game. I wouldn't learn until much later the beautiful truth of God's forgiveness.

If we confess our sins, he is faithful and just to forgive us our sins, and to cleanse us from all unrighteousness (1 John 1:9 KJV).

"We are almost done with this game," one would say, but they rigged it so that the game of Euchre went on and on . . . and on . . . and on.

Chapter Nine

My Parents' Sacrifice

My parents not only paid for my tuition, room, and board, but they also gave me a checking account for emergencies. My first purchase was a ukulele that cost $40.00. I played it every day and got really good at it. A couple of times, I skipped an afternoon class to sit on the sunroof of my dorm and play my ukulele in my two-piece yellow bathing suit.

I had been protected and controlled at home, so I went wild in the freedom of Indiana University. That first semester, a girl named Susan in the dorm, who used to hang out at a place called Sh-t Palace, offered to bleach my hair. Ouch! It stung so badly that she had to take it off too soon. I looked in the mirror. My hair was yellow streaked with pink, years before that was fashionable.

"I'll pierce your ears," said a girl from the fourth floor. She walked in with a cork and a needle and set to work.

"Oh, this hole is lopsided. I need to do it over." Slowly she wiggled an unsterilized needle into my fleshy earlobe and into cork. Oh, it hurt!

The same semester, the Marine took me to a motel for the first time.

"I want to get it over with," I said, believing the lie that I was the only virgin on the floor and I needed to join the ranks.

"You'll be sorry in the morning."

"I don't care. I just want to get it over with."

He complied, and the next morning there was a bloodstain on the bed. I was not sorry. Had not one twinge of guilt. For me, "morning" didn't come until years later.

My precious daddy who adored me, traveled as part of his job and, one day out of nowhere, he showed up in my dorm. The woman at the desk notified our floor that there was a gentleman caller who was coming up. I heard the knock, opened the door, and there was my father at my door. He looked at me and wept. I had been out the night before, so my mascara was all down my face beneath a nest of yellow and pink hair, and I no doubt smelled like cigarette smoke.

My father had tried so to protect me. My continual begging to be with the Marine, my vows that I would marry him, my temper tantrums when they kept denying me the right to see him, had thrown my father into an anxiety attack so that one day he collapsed at work and was taken to the ER with a suspected heart attack. I was sad and scared for my father, but that obsession with the Marine blinded me to all decency. Now that I was away at college, my father could only hope that the relationship between me and the Marine would be a thing of the past with all the interesting young men I was sure to meet.

Footprints

Keep watching and praying that you may not enter into temptation; the spirit is willing, but the flesh is weak (Matthew 26:41 NASB).

Was my spirit willing? Where was that little girl who knelt on the ottoman praying for all little girls who didn't have anyone to pray for her? Where was that thirteen-year-old girl holding her breath watching Jesus' eyes melt into those of the woman who wasn't even in the film? Where was she? In her deceptions and rebellion she was hurting the two people who most loved her in the world. If I could say anything to parents, as I write this, tears streaming down, is, "Don't take your children's hideous behaviors as lack of love for you. Your constant love will reach their hearts."

One day, I received a five-page, single-line handwritten note from my father about the dangers and ultimate disasters that would await me if I continued a relationship with the Marine. I read it, took it to the incinerator chute on the floor, and dropped it down the four floors to the fire below. Oh! How I wish—how I long—to hold those pages today written with his precious hand.

Because I had received good grades in high school without exerting much effort, I never learned to study. It all came easily to me except for math, and I made sure I wasn't going to take math in college. I had wanted to be a psychiatric social worker, but I looked at the requirements, which included statistics, so I switched to psychology. It looked like I could sail through four years of college with no math in order to receive a bachelor's degree in psychology.

But I still loved writing and I couldn't wait to start writing my compositions. I would dazzle that instructor. After all, I was hilarious. Everyone loved my humor and sarcasm.

What a shock! My first composition was handed back. A large red D at the bottom of the last page with lots of red squiggles throughout. What? Cheryl Samelson, National Honor Society, a D? I made an appointment with Mr. Quickpencil.

"Come in. Have a seat."

"Mr. Quickpencil, I received a D on my composition."

"Yes, you have."

"Mr. Quickpencil, I got only As in composition in high school."

A look over bushy brows. "Miss Samelson. This is not high school. Look at the assignment. A descriptive piece of writing describing your dorm room. May I read it to you?"

"Yes."

"'The area beneath the window was blocked by two feet of clothing that had been flung off the bed. The corners of the room were made round by the mounds of cracker crumbs.'

"Miss Samelson, a description is an exact explanation, something that could hold up in court. A bird's-eye view. This is not a description." He went on to explain description as his cigarette-stained hand thumped on the handout we had received.

I walked back to my dorm. Boring. Dull. "The floor is linoleum. The walls are beige" would be insufferably boring to write, never mind to read.

The next assignment was to explain how to prepare a meal. I chose Thanksgiving and made a big production about the turkey being slippery, bouncing off the floor, landing in the dog dish. We stuffed the wrong end, forgot to take the innards out and so, when it was being carved, this blobby bag of yuck squirted out on the guests. I got my paper back. It was hilarious. I knew he would love it. A big red D.

I went back to Mr. Quickpencil.

"Explain. Explain. Explain. These are steps. The first paragraph will lay out what you will explain. Paragraphs two and three will do the explaining. What exactly was done and how. Procedures. Procedures." There went the yellow finger-stub again.

I hated rules and guidelines and structure. I wanted to float freely in my writing. Rules took all the fun out of writing. So I balked. I did it my way paper after paper after paper with D after D after D.

Then I decided to follow the guidelines, and I did exactly what was expected. I received my paper back. In huge red letters: "Miss Samelson, you finally got it! You got an A!"

The A came too late.

The Marine came down to see me on most weekends. When I wasn't going off with him on weekends, I was playing Euchre with the girls or playing my ukulele. The only time I studied was right before a test, and it was disastrous. I would be up all night studying and so exhausted the next day that I couldn't concentrate on the exam. Concentration wouldn't have helped much anyway. Because I wasn't studying efficiently, I didn't know the material. Between my lousy study habits, my sneaking out, and my blasé attitude, it was no wonder that the first semester my grade was 1.9 and I was on academic probation.

When my parents got the letter about my academic standing, I was surprised at their attitude. Instead of shock, my mother said, "We thought you would flunk out of school but wanted to give you a chance."

Not only was my academic standing on the bottom rung of the ladder, but the bit of shredded faith I brought to college had been destroyed in my freshman year. I took Introduction to Theater and got a D. Who can get a D in theater?

"What people came to call the soul was just an explanation of dreams." I sat there, numb, as the theater professor spoke in the tone—and stood in the stance—of an expert, so it made me feel that if I didn't believe it I was an imbecile. "Men went to sleep and saw pictures. To make sense of life and their own worth they came up with the concept of the soul. And some people believe it today." He turned from us snickering as if to add "and what fools they are."

And my Introduction to Anthropology class.

"If you are going to pick mates, be sure to look at their genetic makeup. Those cells, which have evolved to this state, will produce the next generation of the same. If you want a child with slumping posture, who wears glasses and has crooked teeth and is not too bright, then pick a mate accordingly."

The anthropology professor's lectures had the effect of making me see myself as only a body: bones, tissue, cells, genes. The theater professor had convinced me that I had no soul. If I were only a body and had no soul, who would be watching me, caring what I did? Who would be keeping score? No one. Since the theater class and the anthropology lectures destroyed my faith, it must not have been very strong, and you see how rebellious I was, how I did it all my way. There was nothing at all about my life that had a hint of a faithful lifestyle in its fibers.

Fingerpointer

Fingerpointer Satan was hindering the faith of the students by ridiculing God. We had an opportunity to fight it with faith or swallow it. I digested it.

Chapter Ten
God Uses It All

I started the second year on probation. The Marine decided to enroll, and apparently my parents decided it was useless to try to keep us apart. Oddly enough, his being on campus had benefits for me. I made a decision to make studying top priority.

I taught myself a plan of study that I have continued to use. I highlighted my books and took careful notes in class. When I got home from school, I copied my highlighted portions of book text into my notebook. I then went through my notes from class and highlighted and copied those, as well. That boring format the writing teacher had taught me my freshman year? I continued to use that no-fail writing plan all three and a half years of undergraduate work, all through my master's degree courses, and in my theology study. No fail! I taught it to my students.

My senior advanced expository writing class was taught by a professor who had worked for *Newsweek Magazine*. The professor hammered in the phrase, "omit needless words," until they were ingrained.

"Just start writing," he would say, "then chop off the first three paragraphs. There you will find the meat of your text." He shared tips from *Newsweek Magazine*. "Write in such a way that the reader feels he is right there because the details make him see, hear, taste, and smell the environment." Yes, I used those writing techniques from the freshman teacher and senior professor all my life. I finally got it right.

In college, I also learned not to depend on others for my success. Some college professors may have been brilliant, but it didn't mean they could transfer their knowledge into my brain in a way that I could use it. We learned to form study groups when professors were unable to give us information we needed. That began a lifelong practice of being proactive about learning.

"You can't teach me? I will find a way to learn it," was my attitude. I was continually on the lookout to find people who knew more than I did in those classes. Later, I became one of those people who had little groups around me wanting to know what I knew. That lifelong lesson began with the ineffectiveness of someone who was paid to be effective but wasn't. He had a thick foreign accent and taught geography standing with his face six inches from the chalkboard. The two hundred of us sat behind him, staring at his back, while he mumbled incomprehensively to the board. Instead of simply complaining, we became proactive before it was a buzzword. We formed study groups and taught each other what the teacher should have taught us. I learned not to let my negative feelings keep me from a positive outcome.

Footprints

This would become invaluable to me later.

Those hard lessons in my freshman year, and my determination to learn even if no one seemed qualified to teach, kept me persevering when others gave up.

Study to shew thyself approved unto God, a workman that needeth not to be ashamed, rightly dividing the word of truth (2 Timothy 2:15 KJV).

When the Marine came to live on campus, not only did my grades improve, but my faith emerged anew. We studied together instead of running off to hotels. We started attending Hillel together. Hillel is the largest Jewish campus organization in the world. Jews are not out to evangelize non-Jews, but they do very much want to embrace their own with a deep and warm knowledge of Judaism. Hillel is part of a move within Judaism to get secular Jews who attend services only on High Holidays and bring them back into the fold. Hillel meets in more than one hundred colleges and universities and provides a place for Jewish students to explore and celebrate their Jewish identity.

"Cheryl, look at this." The Marine pointed to a poster on the wall of the Hillel foyer.

"Have an adventure! Spend a year in Israel with Sherut La'am, Service to the People." Sherut La'am was an organization formed by the Jewish Agency in Israel to bring North Americans and Europeans to Israel to volunteer for a year. It was similar to the Peace Corps in that it was a year of service but, unlike the Peace Corps, Sherut La'am wasn't helping a developing nation, or what we used to call a third world country. I really think it was a strategy on the part of the Israeli government to give American Jews a taste of Israel and so they would decide to make *aliyah* to come to Israel to settle.

"Do this, Cheryl. It will turn you from a girl into a woman." God used the Marine to mold me in several ways: to honor my religion, to study well and consistently, and to reach toward a new life.

I called my parents and told them about an opportunity to go to Israel with Sherut La'am.

They jumped at the idea. Israel! Anything to get me away from the Marine. I called the number, asked for and received the application in the mail, filled it out, and mailed it, never dreaming that I would be accepted.

I continued going to classes, never skipping anymore, attending Hillel, and practicing for the Mini 500, something the girls in the dorm had roped me into. The mail came. I was accepted! I would leave Indiana for the tiny country of Israel in three months. Everything changed.

The Mini 500 was a tricycle relay race, a cutesy entertainment for the Little 500, Indiana University's annual bike race, the largest collegiate bike race. The men's bike race team consisted of four members in each group, so we girls were four, as well. I, being the smallest, was last and would hop off, straddling my legs to dismount as the trike hurtled ahead. My legs were black and blue. I would miss participating in the actual event because on the weekend of the race I needed to be in Greenwich Village, New York, to meet with my teammates who would be going to serve in Sherut La'am that summer.

I told the girls in the dorm I wouldn't be returning the following year, and I let some of the professors know. By this time, I was an excellent student and felt comfortable with them. In Ballantine Hall I was leaving my American poetry class, which I loved, taught by a professor who made the words of the poets come alive.

"Emily Dickinson brings poetry into the kitchen," was a quote I never forgot. He was a short man whom I pegged as Jewish because of clues that Jews interpret, such as facial features, stature, voice intonation, their choice of conversation topics. I stepped onto the elevator with him.

"I won't be back next year. I'm going to Israel with Sherut La'am." I said it quietly, almost as an understatement. He would have had to strain to hear me. I don't recall ever exchanging a word with this man before this moment on the elevator. His response was undisguised admiration and longing. It made me wonder. What? Why? What would this year hold in store?

What *would* the year hold in store? Maps hung in the walls of Sinai Temple's classrooms on which Israel was a tiny pink slice along a body of water. My parents bought a large world map in preparation for my leaving and put it right above the breakfast bar in the dining room so we would see it at every meal.

What would I be doing months from now? What would it look like? How would people act there? What did the land, the streets, the cities look like? I had never even been to camp. I can't imagine how I mustered the courage to venture out across the world with not one soul I knew and no phone communication. I didn't realize it, but once I set foot on the plane I would not talk to my parents for a year. Or to the Marine. He, however, was losing his hold on me already as I was growing away from him. No—more than growing. In Israel I was going to become *alive* for the first time!

I flew from Bloomington, Indiana, to Chicago on a little plane nicknamed the Blue Goose. Aptly named. It was like flying on the back of a goose. Rocky.

There was room for only four of us in the plane. From Chicago, I flew to New York where someone met me and drove me to our lodgings in Greenwich Village, where all the Sherut La'amniks who had been accepted for the year were to gather for a few days.

I was in a foreign country within my own country. Here were sophisticated young adults from all over the United States and Canada, but mostly from New York. They discussed their jobs or graduate school. I said I was in the midst of practicing for a tricycle race and showed them my bruises. They were shocked when I said I was from Indiana. They didn't know people actually lived there.

I quickly learned that New Yorkers don't conceive of life outside of New York. So I had my first plane ride, drank my first egg cream, met my first New Yorkers. This would quickly be followed by more and more firsts. The year would cost my parents $850.00, which included the airfare and lodging. I would receive $300 per month as a stipend once I got to the city where I would be placed. I was peeling out of my small town Indiana skin and being loaded into a skin that I couldn't recognize because I had never seen it.

After the dizzying weekend in Greenwich Village, I returned to Indiana University and finished my sophomore year as if in a fog, still earning fabulous grades. I cleaned out my room, and my parents drove down to pick me up. We prepared for my June departure to Israel, which gave us a month.

My poor parents. They had just shelled out for two years of college for me while saving for my brother who was supposed to begin the semester after I graduated. I was adding on a double tuition, room and board for them, as well as unforeseen expenses of a daughter living abroad. We bought everything on the list of suggested items including a large trunk, which would later be shipped to me containing things I would need for a year's stay in Israel.

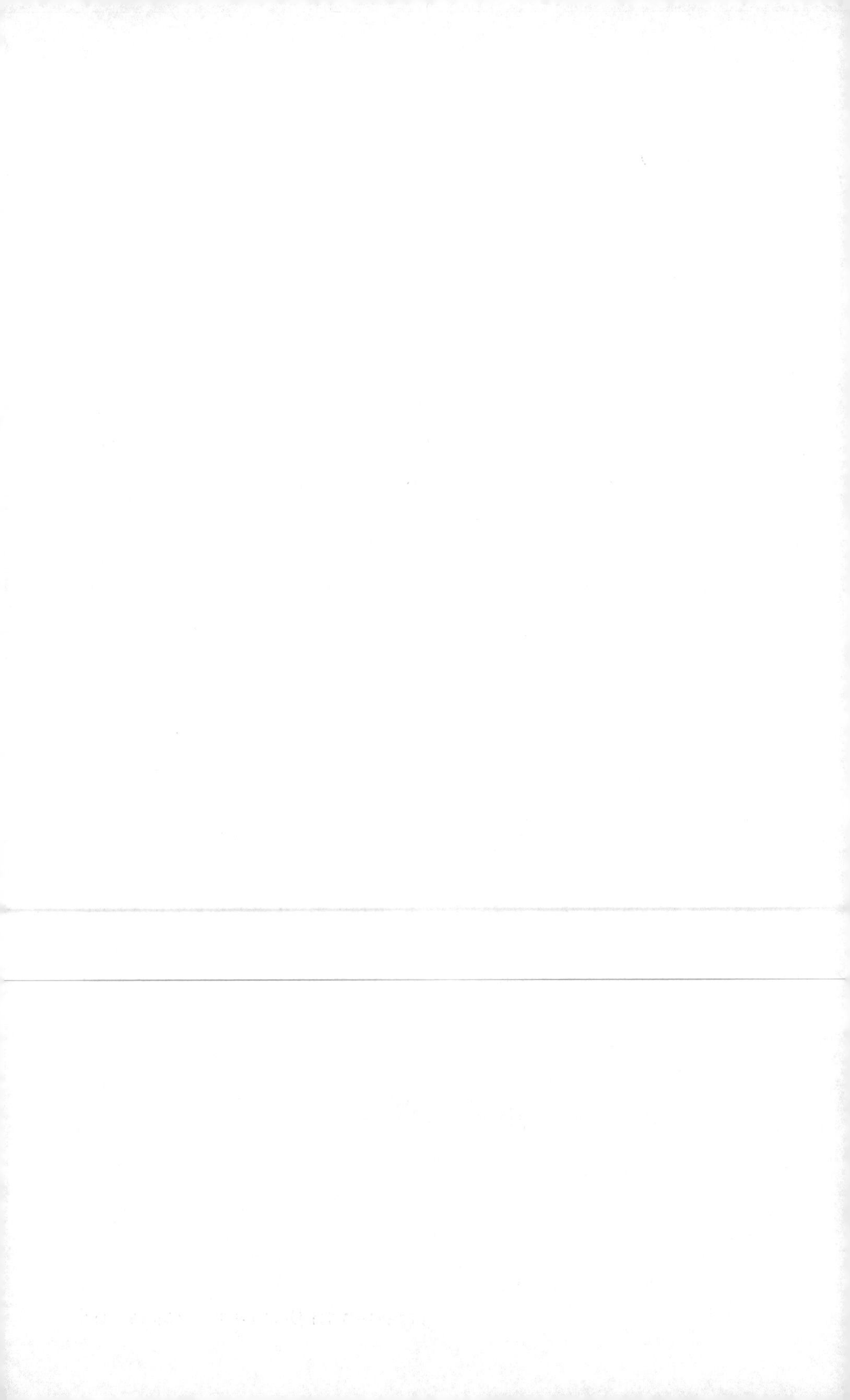

Chapter Eleven
What Was I Doing?

I sat down at the dining room table staring up at that map. Jeff, 15 years old, plopped down next to me.

"Just think, Cheryl. If you die in Israel you'll die among strangers."

At the time when Jeffrey said, "Just think, if you die in Israel you will die among strangers," he was feeling fearful for me. I just thought he was teasing, being the younger brother.

When war broke out near the end of my stay—and those words could have become reality—my love for Israel was so strong that I didn't care.

Nothing prepared me for what lay ahead. Before heading for Israel, we had a week of preparation in South Branch, New Jersey. My parents and the Marine took me to O'Hare Airport and sent me off to South Branch, the first leg of the journey. I sat there, unshed tears welling up as I felt the airplane taxi away from the buildings. A chatty, way-too-happy girl was seated next to me.

"I'm going to New Jersey to learn to be a hair stylist! I am so nervous. What are you doing?"

I stared, not realizing she was talking to me. I mumbled that I was going to Israel for a year.

She pouted. "Everyone does more exciting things than I do."

The plane landed and someone with a sign that said Cheryl Sherut La'am stood at the gate. She helped me with my bag and took me to a large group of people who looked like they were in their twenties. When we were all accounted for, we were taken to a group of vans and driven to a rural area, up a gravel road, and up to a large farmhouse.

"This is it!" our driver said. "Go on in and get your room assignments. Supper will be in the dining room at 6:30."

I walked up the gray steps leading to a veranda that encircled the large house and walked in. I got my room assignment, dropped my things on the bed, and went out to join the other Sherut La'am participants who were heading out toward the steps and sidewalk. One guy sat playing his guitar. Other kids started gathering and sitting below where he was seated on the top step. Strings and voices flowed through the grounds where other groups had walked toward the grass and were sitting under trees. Soon it was 6:30. We all stood up and made our way into the dining room. We took our seats at the long tables and noticed dishes that we came to know as typical Israeli foods. We helped ourselves, chatted, and became quiet as one of the leaders stood up to a microphone.

"We are glad to have members of Sherut La'am's first group with us to give us some directions and help with you, the second group. They will be here all four days telling you what to expect and answering your questions. So now, as you're finishing up dessert I want to call up Gadi and Jonathan."

Two men who looked like college students approached the microphone.

"I don't know what you're expecting, but you're wrong."Gadi, a slender young man with curling shoulder-length hair looked at us with a fierceness in his eyes. "You are going to be lonesome and hot. You are going to be scared, and you will want to go back home. If you have any doubts, now is the time. Sherut La'am is no place for people who are not totally committed to helping *Eretz* Israel." He handed the microphone to Jonathan.

"Today is Sunday. Thursday you leave for Israel. You are going to want to call home and call it quits. It's tough. There is no phone available to you in Israel. Mail delivery takes eight days. By the time you write your parents that hysterical letter about seeing a snake or hating the showers and they write you back, you will be onto another emergency, so do yourselves a favor. Don't write bad stuff. Don't worry them."

With dinner and our pep talk over, I started to think that I needed to make two phone calls, but a Sherut La'am volunteer nudged me. I looked at his name tag.

"Hi, Stan."

"Cheryl, come out in back." Stan was skin and bones, and his huge brown eyes seemed to be all pupils.

"Look up at those stars. Can you see the colors? Can you hear the sounds they are making?" Stan was sent home before we left New Jersey. His psychiatrist had thought the year in Israel would do him good, but the organization apparently thought otherwise. Now, all these years later, with research on sound, light, and movement, I would love to have heard more of what Stan had to say.

I walked to the office and asked to use the phone. I called my mother and then I called the Marine. I told them each the same thing. "If I call you from here in New Jersey telling you to come get me, that I don't want to go to Israel, don't get me! Make me go!" They agreed.

The next afternoon we again gathered on the steps of the big farmhouse. What a mixture of people. South Branch, New Jersey. I had never met people like this.

I was among the youngest. The oldest was thirty-one years old. Some of us were college students and several were already in professions.

Kate was sitting on the porch with a group of us and whipped out a little container and started talking openly about her "diaphragm." Dan, one of the guys in the group was open about his homosexuality, and Kate was determined to change his mind.

"I have my special ways," she said. "Just you wait and see." The only way I'd heard the word diaphragm used in a sentence was when our chorus teacher told us to lift ours in order to deliver the best sound. Always used to speaking up to make my presence known, I tried to think of something to say but couldn't.

The next evening at supper Gadi and Jonathan were there to, once again, discourage the squeamish and timid from going. "Don't expect the kibbutnziks to be grateful for your help. They won't be. You won't be able to speak the language, and even if they speak English they won't let you know. They will do nothing to make it easy for you. They are a hard bunch. Most of the Israelis are not Sabras because the country is so new, and since Sabra, by definition, is an

Israeli Jew born in Israel, there just aren't enough years to produce a generation of Sabras. Sabras have been in 'the Land' since before '48. They're tough. They have been through a lot, and they have little sympathy for soft Americans."

I returned to Israel thirty years later and asked, "Are you a Sabra?"

The answer was, *"Betach!"* of course. What a difference a generation made in a young country.

Supper finished, we once again headed outside for the steps and the porch. Out came the guitar and the folk music. I heard songs I hadn't heard before. In my dormitory at I. U., the Temptations and the Supremes boomed in the snack bar. But these? These songs branded themselves in my brain as a sign of that year. The one that seemed to be our theme song was, "The Times They Are A-Changin," by Bob Dylan. Boy, were they ever!

On the last day, we were once again rounded up.

"Remember the name of the group. Sherut La'am. Service to the people. You are going as a service. Israelis are the people whom you will serve. You will not be thanked. You will not have a car or a phone. You will be lonely."

They did their best to weed out the weak and those without fortitude and staying power. They wanted to dispel any pleasant misconceptions. "If you're going to get cold feet, get it over with. Once you're there, your parents will not bring you home. They have each received a letter from us telling them to disregard any hysteria or cries for help. By the time they receive your crybaby letter, which takes eight days to arrive, you will have gotten over the crisis. So don't disturb your families with the emotional upheaval you are going to experience."

Footprints

This prepared me for life in the kingdom of God.

The guys were saying, "Look, many won't make it. A few do. It's hard. It takes perseverance." Later, as a believer I would learn what it means to "make it to the end."

Don't give up. Don't get weak. Don't let people kick you out of the race.

Keep your eye on the prize. But now, I just knew I wasn't going to give up. No way!

"You will be hated by everyone because of me, but the one who stands firm to the end will be saved" (Matthew 10:22 NIV).

The day before departure, my feet weren't cold. They were ice. I called my parents.

"I changed my mind."

I called the Marine.

"Come get me!"

I had trained them well. "Nope. You are going to get on that plane."

My brother's earlier words were just below the surface of my panic. "Just think. If you die in Israel you'll die among strangers."

Oh, dear. What was I doing?

The next morning was the day of departure. I had one request written down on a piece of paper. My mother asked me to make sure I would visit the *B'nai B'rith* Children's Home, which her B'nai B'rith Sisterhood chapter supported for years.

B'nai B'rith means Sons of the Covenant and is the oldest and largest Jewish service organization in the world. It was established in 1843 and began working to improve the wretched conditions in which Jewish immigrants were living in the New World. The Sisterhood was the organization for women.

Chapter Twelve
To the Land

No turning back now. I boarded the plane, found my seat, and fastened my seatbelt, then wondered if I was the only one seated. The others were on top of the seats. They were sitting *on the backs of the seats!* I was shocked. I couldn't imagine not obeying the seat belt sign. But I looked to the front and to the back. Hardly anyone was in a seat. They must have been so used to traveling and getting their own way, so disregarding of authority that they thought nothing of putting their shoes on the seats and propping their bodies on the backs of the seats. Snug in my seatbelt, I was appalled.

"We are not taking off until everyone is seated." Air France personnel walked up and down the aisles speaking individually to passengers who were still atop the seats.

Finally, everyone complied, and the massive machine managed to get airborne. Until then, I had flown twice—once on the six-seater and then on a slightly larger plane. But this! It was enormous. I had a window seat and did not shut my eyes during the entire flight. I was in awe of the beauty of the skies. We passed sunrise after sunrise after sunrise!

We were able to get off the plane in Ireland when we refueled. I bought a cookbook there for my mother and chatted a bit with some of the volunteers. By this time, everyone had Hebrew names except me. I was standing with one of the young men and said, half to myself, "What should my name be? What is Hebrew for Cheryl?" He cocked his head and looked at me. "I don't know, but I think you look like a Shulamite." Shulamite it was.

Once back on the plane, it was not long before reverent voices whispered, wept, prayed.

"*Eretz Yisroel!*"

Footprints

Oh, the Land! The Land of Israel! The land that was part of the Covenant of God.

My heart yearns for Israel.

***And I will bring again the captivity of my people of Israel, and they shall build the waste cities, and inhabit them; and they shall plant vineyards, and drink the wine thereof; they shall also make gardens, and eat the fruit of them. And I will plant them upon their land, and they shall no more be pulled up out of their land which I have given them, saith the LORD thy God* (Amos 9:14–15 KJV).**

The previously jaunty voices were hushed as we approached the Holy Land. I did not share the sentiments. I wasn't here to see "Holy." I was here to see *Adventure*. While in New Jersey, we were given a survey created by Columbia University. The only question I remember was, "Do you consider yourself first a Jew or first an American?" I didn't have to think twice. With a bold stroke I checked *American*.

The voice of the pilot broke into everyone's hushed conversations.

"We are beginning our descent into Lod Airport, Tel Aviv."

When the plane stopped, we gathered our carry-on luggage and deplaned. Ahead of me, a young man put on his prayer shawl, got off the plane, knelt, and kissed the ground. As I passed him, I scoffed.

"Why are you doing that? You will be here a whole year." I had no reverence for the land. At that time I was a self-centered, foolish girl out to please myself.

Footprints

I scoffed at the young man in the prayer shawl who kissed the ground.

This brings tears to my eyes now—to mock someone's faith. I had let Satan use me.

Knowing this first of all, that scoffers will come in the last days with scoffing, following their own sinful desires (2 Peter 3:3 ESV).

That is such a picture of Satan, the accuser of the brethren, the mocker. I am so sorry!

When we are truly sorry we so want to make things right, to change and never return to that way. First John 1:9 tells us that God not only forgives us, but He cleanses us from unrighteousness. To me that means that He not only said, "I forgive you, Cheryl, for making fun of one of my beloved sons, but I remove from your heart that hate-filled derision for things I love and hold dear."

We collected our luggage and headed outside toward a truck called a tender. Slatted sides bordered the flat bed. There were benches around the sides but not enough for all of us to have seats, so we piled in, some on benches and some on top of luggage. We started out on a highway, then onto smaller roads, and finally up a gravel path leading to a large building resembling a warehouse. We were divided into groups: one group was for the volunteers who were Orthodox. The second group was for those who were not.

I had been raised Reform but had grown to love the richer Conservative traditions in the Hillel House at Indiana University that seemed missing in the Reform. At Hillel, I learned many of the Israeli songs that were sung throughout my year in Israel—songs of the Land, songs of Victory. Some of the Orthodox volunteers would spend their entire year on a *kibbutz* where all the food was kosher and where all the Holy Days were observed.

Since I was not Orthodox, I was sent to *Kibbutz Mishmar Haemek,* a nonreligious *kibbutz*. What an understatement! I found out that God was invited to have no part of life at Mishmar Haemek. It was a shock to think of Israel with no God. It is one thing not to offer kosher foods. But to not even observe the High Holy Days? Not even an acknowledgment of *Shabbat* (Sabbath)?

Chapter Thirteen
More Lies

We were grouped again: professionals and nonprofessionals. The nonprofessionals would do manual labor, and the professionals would work in their professions after finishing our time in *ulpan*. Ulpan is an intense study of Hebrew for new immigrants. While on the *kibbutz*, we studied four hours a day six days a week for four months. The *kibbutz* is a communal settlement established in 1909 for the protection of the Jewish communities, and they continue today to be models of social and economic well-being.

Even though I had just completed my sophomore year, I stood in the line of the professionals because I knew I did not want to work in unskilled labor. One more lie. It seems as if lies were at many turning points of my life, until I turned to the One who is the Truth.

The plan was that we would all go to *kibbutzim*, and from there some of the Orthodox group would stay on the *kibbutz* for the entire year while the rest of us would spend months on a *kibbutz* to attend ulpan and then be sent to a city, town, or village. Ulpan was developed in 1948 to teach Hebrew to the immigrants who streamed into Israel from all over the world, each learning from their native tongues. Ulpan is intense and done through immersion. In the four months that we were in ulpan we never heard one word spoken in English.

After the time in ulpan, I would be sent to Ashdod, a development town. Development towns were built in outlying areas of Israel in the 1950s to absorb the thousands of Jewish immigrants who came in from Arab countries. Most people know about the European Holocaust, but there was persecution elsewhere, as well. Development towns were built to ease the population swell in the center of Israel. Ashdod was made up of mostly Jews who had escaped persecution from Arabic countries in North Africa—Morocco, Tangiers, and Algiers, as well as from Iraq, Iran, and Kurdistan. My job would be to teach English in junior and senior high school. I had left Indiana University at the end of my sophomore year as a psychology major. I had not even taken one class in education because I had no desire to be a teacher.

Perhaps the reason I didn't want to be a teacher was because that is what my father wanted for me. My rebellious desire was to go a different way than the one suggested by my parent. But my father knew best, because teaching is my predominant spiritual gift and I have loved teaching now all these decades.

We piled back into the tenders and were driven to our respective *kibbutzim*. It was dark when we pulled into the *kibbutz* so we were not able to see the regal rows of palm trees bordering the stone-covered path leading to the *heder ha ohel* (dining room) where a meal was set for us at *Kibbutz Mishmar Haemek*. We had a lovely welcome by the *kibbutz* with bread, fresh fruits, vegetables, and chocolate. We were shown to our rooms.

We walked the paths to the small white buildings that held the rooms which would be home. Walking in, we saw two straw cots and a small table on which was a small plate of cookies and chocolates.

Outside was a sink for washing faces and brushing teeth. No need to wash dishes. All of our meals would be in the *heder ha ohel*.

A path led sharply up to our toilets and showers. My roommate was Gina, a sparkling young woman from Texas, who would find her husband in Israel and take him back with her after our year was finished. Gina and I settled into our small room. Our trunks from home would not arrive for five months, so we just had the items that we brought with us and those that were issued to us by the *kibbutz*. Nothing else would have fit in the room anyway.

The next day, we gathered in the dining room to find out about procedures. First we were issued everything we would need for life in the *kibbutz* from clothing to toiletries. *Kibbutz* life at the time was the "ideal" form of communism. No one owned anything. Next, we had to find the jobs to which we would each be assigned: in the kitchen, the laundry, the orchard, the farm, the plastics factory, or janitorial work. Then we were able to take a couple of hours to explore. The *kibbutz* grounds seemed vast. There was a farm with machinery and animals; orchards, vegetable gardens, a little post office, the school classrooms, and expanses of grass.

We learned by observation about the living arrangements of the *kibbutz*. The couples lived in small apartments within larger buildings that looked like white houses built on levels and divided into little one-bedroom spaces.

The children did not live with their parents. A couple days after birth, the babies were moved into a baby house. After that, toddlers lived with toddlers, preschoolers with preschoolers, and so on up until middle school. When the children were teenagers, they were placed four in a room: two boys and two girls. The teens living together was a shocker. We found out that they considered each other like siblings, so marriage among the youth in the same *kibbutz* was rare. The baby house had a sound system with a monitor that could be heard outside. At night a watchman went around the *kibbutz* listening. If he or she heard crying at the baby house, the baby would receive care. No adult stayed with any of the children in any of the houses. The children all slept alone with the sound monitor as security.

Every week, we had to check the work schedule to find out our assignments, which were designated by the *kibbutz menehel* (manager). Schedules varied. Most workers started their day at 5:00 a.m. Some workers started at 4:00 a.m. During the afternoon, the *kibbutzniks* had a long rest from 1:00 to 4:00. But we Sherut La'amniks couldn't rest because we had four hours of Hebrew in ulpan in the afternoon. Even after supper, we couldn't rest because we had three hours of lectures and discussion about the history and present day issues of Israel from 7:00 to 10:00 p.m.

So, first to get our necessities. In the laundry, we were each given bloomers that looked like the ones we wore in Fanny Sebesta's physical education class in high school; sandals and work boots; simple shirts; and little blue hats which looked like sailor hats but with the sides turned down. We were then given our work assignments. I would work in the plastics factory on the *kibbutz*. Arrive outside the *heder ha ohel* at 5:00 a.m., ride the tender the short distance to the factory, work until 7:00 a.m., return to the *heder ha ohel* for breakfast, back to the factory until noon, and to the *heder ha ohel* for lunch.

Breakfast was always the same: cucumbers, green peppers, onions, olives, tomatoes, and a white cool creamy mixture they called *labne*, which was something like a combination of yogurt and sour cream. It was mixed with the vegetables we finely chopped. We also had thick tan bread, hardboiled eggs, and coffee. The coffee was served in glass cups, so it was easy to see the thick black paste that settled in the bottom. We were never offered milk. That was kept in a huge metal vat outside the dining room and was off-limits to everyone except children. It was straight from the cow, had little clumps in it, and was room temperature. Lunch was something of a mystery. We never knew what the meat was. There was always soup of some kind and thick, sturdy bread. Evening meals were always similar to breakfast with perhaps sardines added. At every meal there was a *seebooreet* in the middle of the table—the *kibbutzniks* said it meant, "little public thing"—into which we all threw our scraps. Mondays were ice cream nights, which was a treat. Friday night meant dark, thick, room-temperature beer.

Because it was a nonreligious *kibbutz*, there was no welcoming in the Sabbath Queen. Whereas, at home I was mildly annoyed that I couldn't go to the basketball or football games that fell on Friday night, now I was beginning to see the beauty in awaiting and welcoming the Sabbath Queen, that quiet time where dusk falls and all activity in the home stops in honor of the Queen or Bride of the Sabbath.

Instead of an evening ushering in Shabbat, Friday on *Kibbutz Mishmar Haemek* was a night of fun and dancing. The tables were pushed away after supper, and an accordion player set the atmosphere. *Kibbutzniks* knew how to have fun! They sang and danced in wild circles until late into the night. We Sherut La'amniks joined in with enthusiasm. The music was nationalistic—

loud and spirited songs about the victory of Israel, the virtues of the Haganah and the Palmach. "*Anu Anu Ha Palmach!" (We are the Palmach! A popular song of Israeli statehood.)*

The Haganah was the loose defense force that kept Israel safe from1920–1948, the year Israel became a state. The Palmach was the striking force, an underground military operation. The *kibbutzniks* were very proud of the men and women who guarded and fought for the existence of Israel.

We awoke to routines and lessons. One of the first things we were taught was how to wash a floor Israeli style. This was the first time in my life I had washed a floor at all, and it was great. A floor washing adventure! For me a novelty. We were given a bucket, a squeegee, some liquid cleaner, and a rag. We squirted a little cleaner into the bucket of water, poured a small pool of water on the floor, wrapped the rag around the squeegee, and then sloshed the rag-wrapped squeegee around until an area was full of sudsy water. We repeated the pour-slosh, pour-slosh until the entire floor was full of sudsy water. We then emptied out the bucket and filled it with clear water and repeated the process. After this we squeezed out the rag and set it aside. Taking the squeegee, we carefully squeegeed out the whole floor. There was a drain in the middle of the floor into which we would scrape the water from each side of the room. Everyone washed floors every day.

Why was it my first time washing a floor? Remember my mother? She so wanted me to have every benefit that she never requested I do any chores beyond setting the table and making my bed on weekends. She wanted me to live graciously. That was a phrase I would hear all my life until leaving home to get married: "gracious living."

That evening we took our toothbrushes and washcloths and cleaned up outside under the stars, as we would every night. We lay on our straw cots and tried to get comfortable. It was hot and the windows were open. Beyond the windows were 2,000 chickens and we soon learned that chickens stink! The wind brought the stench through our room and it lingered.

Morning came early. At 4:00 a.m., I put on my rubber shower shoes, took my towel and clothing, and walked up the hill under the stars. After a shower, I dressed, left my hair wet, and headed for the dining room, where other Sherut La'amniks and *kibbutzniks* were gathered for the morning of work. We hopped up into the tender. It jostled along the ruts of the *kibbutz* until we got to our stops. Mine was the factory, so I was helped down and led to my position. The plastics factory made toilet seats, and my job was to examine each disk that went on the toilet seat. There were four bins into which I was to toss the disks based on 1) excellent, 2) good, 3) fair, and 4) unacceptable. At about 6:30 we had a break for cookies and the same thick coffee we were served on the *kibbutz*. I had never been so bored in my life as day after day I took my spot on the stool and separated plastic disks. After a while I made a game of it, creating a little Latin rhythm as I tossed the disks into their bins. "Tatatatata*ta*!"

Within two weeks of our arrival on the *kibbutz*, we were each assigned a *kibbutz* family. My parents were Ehud and Shula, and they were adorable. He was short, strong, and dark. She was light with blonde hair. (Yes, there are blond Israelis.) They had two children, Ori and Sharoni. Ehud had been raised on a *kibbutz*, so it was his life. He was used to the fact that families were separated. When *kibbutzim* were formed, it was a matter of protection. Every man and woman had to work and had to protect the *kibbutz* from hostile intruders. The *kibbutz* plan of separating the children to be raised in children's houses apart from the parents was to facilitate the plan of protection. Removing the distraction and the burden of caring for the children freed every man and woman so the *kibbutz* could function and be protected. By 1966, the chores were still divided among all the adults. Women had equal rights, responsibilities, and status as men. It was communism—as in idealistic communal living—everything evenly shared, everyone having everything in common. Everyone was equally able to work because no one was home with children.

Shula had been raised in a town. Having her children separated from her was a source of anguish.

"I wake up in the middle of the night with my heart beating so hard. I just know my babies are frightened or sick or hurt! I run out of my house as fast as I can to the children's houses and always Ori and Sharoni are sleeping peacefully."

The *kibbutz* parents, even those raised on *kibbutzim*, long for and cherish their children. The most awaited, the most wonderful, the most magical time of the day was the hour of the children. At 4:00, I walked with Ehud and Shula to the children's houses. The children were delighted to see their parents, calling out, *"Eema! Abba!"* as they saw Mommy and Daddy in the doorway. The little families then headed back to their homes. Ori held Ehud's hand. Sharoni, age three, was held in her mama's arms.

"Why do you always carry her?" I asked.

Shula looked at me with sad eyes. "I see my children only two hours a day. I have to make the most of it. I cherish my children and long for them every minute of every day that they are not with me."

Once outside Shula's and Ehud's home, we spread a big blanket on the lawn and set out drinks, fruit, and biscuits for tea. During those two hours, there was never talk of work or friends or world affairs. Eyes and hearts were locked on the children. After tea, we took Ori and Sharoni back to the children's houses where they would have their supper and be put to bed. Once the children were settled, we went back for supper in the *heder ha ohel.*

Years later, I went back to Israel and longed to visit the *kibbutz*, to see Ehud and Shula. I wrote to the *kibbutz*. Ehud, himself, wrote back to me saying that he was now the *kibbutz* manager. A year passed between the time I wrote the letter and actually got to the *kibbutz*. I found out where he lived and ran up to his doorway.

I greeted him with enthusiasm but saw none coming back toward me. I looked at a man shrunk with despair, eyes void of any light.

"Shula," he said, his face marked with pain, "died of cancer three months ago."

Ehud didn't even know me! Here he was stamped on my heart, yet he didn't remember me. In my mind Ehud was in Technicolor, in blazing brilliance. I could close my eyes and see his smile, hear his rugged laugh, as he would say proudly in English, "I am now going to wash my body." But his memory of me had slipped out of his mind like an unnoticed cat leaving through a crack in the fence. Add that to my sorrow over Shula and I was completely heartbroken. I thought of all those hours every day she wept for her children, and now they surely were weeping for her.

My job didn't last long at the plastics factory. After a couple of weeks of not impressing the factory manager, I was reassigned. I went to look at the chart to see where I was working and I saw "public toilets." I went to the laundry lady to get the additional clothing I would need. She handed me rubber gloves that hung off my fingers and big yellow galoshes that were truly five sizes too big because I wear a size 1 (or 31 in Israeli size) and these were the typical 36. The next morning I woke at 5:00 and set out on foot to wash all of the public toilets on the *kibbutz*. There were toilets in the kitchen, the factories, the farm buildings, the schools, the babies' and children's houses, and the teenagers' quarters. I was to clean them all every day. Hygiene products that we took for granted in the United States in 1966 were not available on the *kibbutz*. Plumbing was not of the same efficiency either. Daily, I faced feces and blood in every bathroom. Men must have just squatted over the stool and hoped for the best because the product of the squat was everywhere, and I had to clean it up. Women did not have sanitary pads. They used wads of cloth that they would leave for me to touch and decide whether to throw away or take to the laundry. I would go to the teenagers' quarters with my mop and squeegee, and in my big boots I would shuffle across the sidewalk that connected the rooms. I would go from bathroom to bathroom cleaning showers, sinks, and toilets. Inevitably, one irate teenager would poke a head out of the door (usually a female) and shout, "*Sheket*! Quiet! We are sleeping."

It is a good thing that we had "the talk" in South Branch, New Jersey, warning us how rude and ungrateful the *kibbutzniks* would be. It was as if they wanted to see how much we North Americans could take. Because of the warning I was determined to be gracious (thank you, Mother) and did everything with a smile.

Footprints

Here is a wonderful Scripture being worked out on the inside of me before I knew it. Amazing how much the Word does in our hearts even when we don't know how it got there.

And whatever you do, do it heartily, as to the Lord and not to men (Colossians 3:23 NKJV).

One day, I headed up a path to a building I had not noticed before on the map of my route. I opened the door, went into the bathroom, and started scrubbing. I heard a noise, like blankets moving, and I looked around the corner. There was a man and woman in bed. Who was more shocked? I found out that I had inadvertently entered a private dwelling. So ended my job cleaning bathrooms.

Chapter Fourteen

How Can You Say You're a Jew?

The next day, I reported to the *kibbutz* manager to receive the job I would have for the rest of my stay—working in the orchards splicing fruit trees. Working in the orchards was a beautiful outdoor job and a learning experience on several levels. We stopped at 7:00 for a delicious breakfast cooked outside on an open fire, worked until noon, and then headed back for lunch. I loved working in the orchards.

For my job, I squatted on the ground beneath the bending figure of a young man above me. He made a little slit in the tender trunk of the new tree. Into the slit he placed the seed that would make the tree a peach or pear tree. I would then take the piece of plastic I held in my hand and wrap it tightly around the seeded slit and tie it. We moved centimeter by centimeter down the row—him moving with rhythmic steps, me doing a squatting hop.

"I don't understand how you can say you are a Jew and not believe in God," I said in between squatting hops.

Without stopping he snorted. "If we waited for God to build this land we'd still be in exile."

"But God! The whole definition of a Jew is someone who believes in one God," I argued.

He stopped. "Says who? *Says who*? So you're a Jew? How can you be a Jew if you don't live in Israel?"

That was a puzzlement. So these atheistic *kibbutzniks* believed that to be a Jew one had to live in Israel. I, and every Jew I knew in the USA, said that to be Jew you have to worship the God of Abraham, Isaac, and Jacob.

What a metaphor for me. Splicing fruit trees! The tree was just a tree, not planning to bear any fruit. But hands reached down, made a slit—no doubt a painful slit—and inserted the tiny seed that determined what kind of tree it was, what kind of fruit it would bear. The tree had nothing to do with choosing its own fruit—and once borne, the fruit wouldn't be for itself, but for the consumption, the pleasure, the nutrition of others.

 Footprints 

God said to Moses, "I AM WHO I AM," and He said, "Thus you shall say to the sons of Israel, 'I AM has sent me to you.'" God, furthermore, said to Moses, "Thus you shall say to the sons of Israel, 'The LORD, the God of your fathers, the God of Abraham, the God of Isaac, and the God of Jacob, has sent me to you. This is My name forever, and this is My memorial-name to all generations (Exodus 3:14–15 NASB).

After lunch, while the *kibbutz* slept, we had our four-hour Hebrew class. We enjoyed teasing our Hebrew teacher. Benjamin never once spoke English. Nothing would get him to speak to us in English or acknowledge our whining or begging. Oh, Benjamin! In his rumpled shorts, sandals, and shock of white hair he was endearing. He lapsed one time out of his Hebrew, but not into English. Over and over again, he gave us a clue or a pantomime to help us to understand the word he was trying to teach us. Impossible. None of us had a clue. Then, sighing, he said, *"Le schlepp."* In unison we all shouted, "To drag!" We all knew that much Yiddish.

Hebrew is an ancient language revived by a man named Eliezer Ben Yehudah whose goal was "only Hebrew all the time everywhere." For Americans who aren't used to speaking more than one language, it was a challenge. Some of the group had studied Hebrew in synagogue, and they were at a disadvantage. I knew nothing, so I was a clean slate not having to unlearn anything, unlike those who had learned the Ashkenazi Hebrew where *t*'s sound like *s*'s and the accent is on a different syllable.

I'm very social, so I spent lots of time conversing with the *kibbutzniks*. I loved talking to them even with my few words. One idea Benjamin gave us, which I used constantly, was to carry around a *pinkus* (little notebook), and every time I heard an interesting word I asked what it was and what it meant. I transliterated it, that is, wrote it phonetically so I could reproduce it in speech. Benjamin actually used me as an example, "Be like Shula. She doesn't care if she's right or wrong. She just talks."

This later characterized my walk with the Lord, as well. I developed an enormous boldness as a believer in Jesus and just *did it*. Others would wait until they could do it right. I just *did it* and learned much about functioning in the kingdom of God on the run.

From our classroom, it was a short walk to the post office. Those little blue aerogrammes were beacons of joy. I waited until I got back to my room to carefully open them to read every word written by someone who remembered me.

After Hebrew class, we returned to our rooms to drop off our books and hurry for that magical children's hour with our "families." After supper, more relaxing hours awaited the *kibbutzniks* unless their chores involved cleaning the kitchens. Imagine being a married couple with children and having absolutely no responsibilities in the evening. No helping children with homework, no listening to them squabble, no arguing over TV shows. The couples on the *kibbutz* simply enjoyed quiet in their dwellings or strolls on the beautiful paths. No peaceful rest for us Sherut La'amniks because, immediately after supper, we were in a meeting room learning—always learning—more about Israel.

Those were long tiring days. Our obligations were not finished until 11:00 at night and some of the Sherut La'amniks set their alarms at 3:00 a.m. to be at work by 4:00. In fact, two New York girls were on that 4:00 a.m. schedule requiring the 3:00 a.m. alarm.

"I'm not used to coming in from dates until 3:00," one wailed.

It was definitely a new way of life. I immersed myself in learning the language; the new culture, which I was growing to love; getting to know my family, whom I quickly learned to adore, including a *sabba* and *safta* (grandpa and grandma) who also lived on *Kibbutz Mishmar Haemek*. I was busy and happy. I didn't notice a few of our Sherut La'am girls were sneaking out at night with men of the *kibbutz*.

Mishmar Haemek, as a nonreligious *kibbutz*, did not adhere to religious ceremonies, like weddings. The men and women sharing homes were not called *ba'al v' eesha* (man and wife) because those two words actually mean *ba'al*, owner, and *eesha*, woman. Instead, those couples—parents of the children they picked up every day—were called *haverim* (friends). So, perhaps, the fact that one of the "friends" sneaked out at night with one of our women was a casual matter. While we were there, one *kibbutz* couple swapped. He moved out, she moved in, and they were new *haverim* without blinking an eye.

The Scandinavian volunteers loved the sun, so they would be sure to work in the orchards (wonder how they got to choose) and rumor had it that they would take off their shirts and pick fruit in their bras. The *kibbutz* men flocked to the orchard when the Scandanavian girls were out there. No ceremonies also meant no *Shabbat*. Yes, Friday evening came followed by Saturday which was *Shabbat*, but there were no candles, no prayers, no *Shabbat Shalom*. It was another day except for the music and dancing.

At the end of the first month, we were each assigned a family from a nearby city or town—families who had applied to have a North American "adopted" son or daughter for the duration of our *kibbutz* stay.

"Here are the names and addresses of your town families. You are responsible for finding your transportation. Your family has been notified that they were chosen to be your family, but they have no idea who you are or when you are coming. There is no phone for you to use, so I hope you are able to find them at home."

My poor sense of direction had gotten no better since the days of trying to find my way home from third grade at Edgewood School. I was given nothing but a street address in a town. I had no phone number—or phone—so one day, I just set out alone on the road and headed for the bus station in Afula. I handed the man at the ticket counter the address, and he pointed to a bus. When I climbed up the steps, I handed the driver my paper. My two months of Hebrew did not lend themselves well to questions and absolutely none to comprehending answers. The bus driver nodded and pointed to the seat behind and to the right so he could let me know when to get off the bus.

He caught my eye and lifted a finger toward the door of the bus and beyond toward a house. I thanked him, stepped off the bus and looked at the house the driver indicated before he drove off. I walked up to the door and knocked. A woman opened the door and registered surprise to see a young woman standing in the doorway with a suitcase.

"*Anee po.*" (I am here.) The woman seemed to put two and two together and remembered the agreement she had made. But her face registered a touch of dismay. So, we have the woman, a teacher of *gan yeledim* (kindergarten); her husband, a big wheel in top-secret jobs in the Israeli government; a girl, 17; and a boy, 10.

We got acquainted and, after supper, they showed me where I would sleep on a small pull-out bed in the girl's room. I got my pajamas on, and the boy's face showed amazement. He had never heard of anyone changing clothes to sleep, particularly into cute PJs that had been given to me as a going away gift from one of the Sinai Sisterhood ladies. Things were different then. Now, surely, there are pajamas, but at the time, one dress hung in Ephrat's closet and surely no night garments. I lay down and slept . . . and slept and slept. By nature, I am an early riser. My mother had to order me not to get out of bed until the street lights went off. As an adult, I have to make myself stay in bed until 5:00 a.m.

But on that first night away from the *kibbutz* and its rigorous schedule, I slept until 1:00 in the afternoon. I was so embarrassed.

For some time, I spent every weekend with my city family. As my welcome, there was Penina rolling out dough onto which she sprinkled chocolate and sugar. She rolled it up, popped it in the oven, and—*voila*—there was a streusel. I wanted to be a help to the family—had always been taught by my mother to be a help in other homes and not expect to be waited on. Once I offered to cut the tomato. I started to cut it into wedges, the way we did at home.

"No!"Penina sputtered. "That is no way to open a tomato!"

Then, I suggested frying chicken.

"No! No one fries chicken. What an idea! It would never get done. Chicken must be baked."

On occasion, Penina took me to work with her on her Vespa, a motorbike with an adjacent seat. I enjoyed spending the days with the children at the *gan yeledim* (kindergarten). I noticed one little boy who had recently emigrated from Great Britain. I asked him some questions in English, and he refused to answer.

"It was traumatic for him coming here, not being able to communicate in Hebrew, so now he refuses to revert to English at all," Penina told me.

My hosts took me on weekend trips with them and made me a member of the family. I remembered the promise I made to my mother. So on one of our outings, we drove to the B'nai B'rith Children's home, which Sinai Temple Sisterhood had been supporting as long as I remembered. I was surprised to find that it was not for impoverished orphans as I had assumed. It was for Israeli families who could afford to pay to send their children with disabilities for education and training at a boarding school. I took pictures as promised.

A wonderful side outing was to a gorgeous ancient village built into rocks that jutted into the Mediterranean Sea. Those were warm, wonderful times, and I drew very close with the family.

All was well, except for the father's actions. I was so stupid. I didn't realize that he had anything up his sleeve. But there was one time where I started to get a glimpse.

"Shula, come! We are invited to a party." He started moving to the door. I immediately saw all kinds of movements from behind me and heard hisses.

"Ephrat! *M'hair!"* ("Ephrat, hurry!") Ephrat, struggling to get into her one dress, rasped out, *"Goal nefesh!"* which means something that utterly disgusts one's soul.

I started for the first time to realize why Penina was so dismayed to see a young woman come to the door with a suitcase.

"Shula, you are very beautiful," the father whispered to me in the car where we were waiting for Ephrat.

"Are you a *wurchin*?"

I got it! The man was a pervert. Would my father ever ask one of my girlfriends if she were a virgin? Thank God, his daughter walked out, and that was the last time I allowed myself to be alone with the dad. I kept my distance and soon stopped going for weekends altogether.

Chapter Fifteen
Seeing the Land

The *Sachnut* (Jewish Agency) had tours planned for us as part of the $850 fee of participating in Sherut La'am for the year. We piled into the bus and headed to our first tour, an area between Mishmar Haemek and Haifa. I did not want to stay bunched in a group of Americans and listen to a tour guide. One of the girls in our group who was bilingual, translated for her, but she was rude and blasé. If the tour guide spoke for three minutes, the translator sighed, rolled her eyes, and spoke six words in a flat tone. I wanted to move and to see. I wanted to experience. I wanted to be around the people. I wanted reality. I wanted a genuine experience, not a classroom lecture. I motioned to a girl to follow me and I led her away from the group.

We came upon a low, rectangular building surrounding a courtyard. As we approached, a woman with a basket in her arms saw us and smiled then turned quickly and ran toward the house. Two men emerged and gestured, welcoming us into their home. Their faces broke into wide smiles as they waved us in and gestured that we be seated on high couches while the woman scurried off for coffee to serve us. Our gazes took in the room. Every wall was covered with a colorful, wildly decorated thick piece of material, none matching. The woman returned with a tray and tiny cups. I patted the seat next to me and urged her to sit, but she shook her head and wagged her finger. Apparently it was not allowed or appropriate. The coffee was unlike anything I have put into my mouth before or since. I had to strain it through my teeth because it felt as if there were bits of pungent, flavorful bark in it.

What a blessing. How generous and welcoming. We found that they were Druze. The woman was such a dear. On the way out, I asked if I could photograph her. A vigorous, simultaneous shaking of the head and fingers and fast retreat into a back room. I didn't know that conservative Druze consider photographing a woman dishonors her and that the government even issues waivers for the identification of Druze women—no picture.

But I did learn that *no* is no in any language. Our bus took us to the next location, and we stepped off onto the pavement. From even far off, we could hear glorious music coming from a group of brown-robed men. I walked toward them to tell them how much I loved the sound, but one of the men made an angry face in absolute contrast to the beauty of the voices and shooed me away with unmistakable robe-clad arm thrusts. Another "no" in any language.

Later that evening, we reached Mount Tabor. I stood on the mountain looking out at the expanse of rock as far as I could see—peaks of differing shapes in varying shades of gray. I could imagine Deborah the Judge looking up at the heavens, seeing the same brilliant stars that I saw. What an awesome moment. The vastness of God. The memories of those stars, of that mountain seem to be stored in my cells. I can bring the sight back on demand and feel the same awe. The marvel of visual memories.

And, of course, there was the desert, the Negev. I had assumed that all deserts were made of sand. The Negev was not. It was rock. *Rock.* Hard, unyielding, hot rock. The tour was definitely for the young and fit. We had to crawl on our bellies and elbows through narrow, skinny, dark passageways.

Tours were spread throughout the four months we spent on the *kibbutz*, but into our third month, we were approaching the High Holy Days, and we were in a dilemma.

Because *Kibbutz Mishmar Haemek* was a nonreligious *kibbutz* and, therefore, did not acknowledge God at all, *Rosh HaShana* and *Yom Kippur* were ordinary days. This seemed crazy. Here we were, Jewish youth and young adults who had come to Israel, which was the epitome of *Jewish*, and the *kibbutz* didn't even acknowledge the *One* who made us Jewish? The One God—the God of Abraham, Isaac, and Jacob? We had become used to the fact that Friday night was not a time to have challah and wine, say the *Kiddush* and the *Hamotze* (blessing over the wine and bread), and think about God, but instead it was party night with lively circle dancing and accordion playing. It seemed that the god of the *kibbutz* was *Eretz Yisroel*.

But this was the season of the High Holy Days. We went to the *kibbutz* leaders. "We need to go to town. We need to observe the High Holidays."

"No. It will be a work day. You have chores. You will stay and work. It is just a day."

"That's not right. It's against our beliefs. We have a right to go to High Holiday services. It's wrong that you stop us."

Back in the USA, if anyone had told me that, one day, I would stage a rebellion to be *allowed* to go to synagogue on the High Holy Days, I'd think they were nuts. Jewish kids were excused from school on *Rosh Hashana* and *Yom Kippur*, but it was not "fun." It was a day of fasting and sitting for twelve hours in services in Hebrew with (in our case) a Gentile cantor droning on and on. I guess we didn't have any Jewish people in our community who had good voices so they hired a singer. It hadn't seemed right, a non-Jewish cantor. But here I was, fiercely claiming my rights to go to synagogue.

The *kibbutz* leaders caved in. We took a bus and arrived before Shabbat in a town called Nazareth Illit, which was formed in 1957 as a Jewish town overlooking Arab Nazareth. We walked through winding paths and noticed that every now and then there was a small opening with sounds of chanting that we recognized as Jewish prayers. We approached one such opening. There was nothing on that stone building indicating that it was a *shul*—no Star of David. No sign. The word *shul* means school in Yiddish, the language of Eastern European Jews. The synagogue is such a place of learning that they lovingly called their synagogue Shul. Peeking in, we saw men swaying and so we started to enter.

Women from inside rushed toward us and started motioning us females backward with sounds of horrified indignation. We young ladies had no head coverings and would not be allowed entrance. Fortunately, one girl in our group spoke Yiddish.

"We are *maidlech*. We are not married. We don't need head coverings."

The guys had no such problem, and they had entered immediately and joined the Israeli men swaying and shouting the prayers with gusto while we girls, allowed in after them, stood behind a heavy curtain and remained silent throughout the long hours of the service.

We spent the night in a small stone home and broke the fast with a family, sharing sardines from a can; then it was back to the *kibbutz*, back to work and studies . . . until I got sick.

When I arrived at the *kibbutz* I was overweight from the high-starch diet at Indiana University. But this sickness was affecting both ends and I was losing weight, so much weight that I was put into the *kupat holeem* (hospital). I was glad to get away from the awful smell of 2,000 chickens wafting into our open window, which hadn't helped the nausea. It was in the *kupat holeem* that I got another look at life on the *kibbutz*. I was rooming with a woman named Sasha, a Russian Jew who had a baby and was due to go home in two days.

"Sasha! You get to take your baby home in two days."

There was a silence. Sasha just looked at me and, with a jolt, I realized that no, she would not be taking her baby home. Babies were immediately removed from the hospital and moved to the baby house. Sasha just stared at nothing, and I felt my heart squeeze for her. Thankfully *kibbutz* women were encouraged to breast feed and were given regular times during the day to leave their chores to go to a common spot to nurse with the other mamas.

Recovered, I returned back to my little straw mattress and 2,000 chickens. Peri, a friend of mine, got sick, but her illness was a more serious case. She was diagnosed with hoof and mouth disease. Her fever always spiked really high at about 4:00. One day, I skipped ulpan to visit Peri and cheer her. When I got back to the school building, I discovered that photographers had been there to take pictures of all the Sherut La'amniks in class and at their work sites, but Peri and I were not in them. The *kibbutz* had sent a photographer to surprise us by taking our photos and putting them into little albums for us. Choices. I had chosen to skip school and spend the afternoon with a sick friend.

The *kibbutz* stay came to an end, and there was a celebration for us in the *heder ha ohel.* Each of us came forward for our certificates and grades from the ulpan. When I walked forward, there was a huge cheer from the *kibbutzniks.* I had spent so much time with the *kibbutzniks*. I would walk around with my little pinkus asking questions, jotting down vocabulary words, and loving the healthy, wholesome *kibbutz* life.

I loved the *Aruchat Arbah*, the 4:00 meal that was the family lawn time. Any moments not swallowed up in work, ulpan, and evening meetings, I was everywhere, visiting everyone every day.

My grade on the ulpan however, was disgraceful. I got *maspeek b'koshi*, which means barely enough—or squeezed by—or passed by the skin of my teeth. Well, as Benjamin had said, "Shula doesn't care if she's right; she just talks." But by the time we left Israel I was probably the most fluent; I even dreamed in Hebrew. I totally immersed myself in the lives of Israelis, spending scant time with Americans. Interestingly now, all these years later, my oral Hebrew is still passable, and I use written Hebrew regularly in the Bible studies I write.

Early the next morning, I ran through the *kibbutz*, hugging friends I had met and particularly said a tearful goodbye to *Sabba* and *Safta* (grandpa and grandma) with whom I had spent many an *Aruchat Arba*. Then, it was over to the *heder ha ohel* where we had schlepped all of our belongings. Mine filled one small satchel because, like everyone else's, my trunk was still en route in the ocean somewhere.

Chapter Sixteen

Off to Ashdod

We loaded everything onto tenders and climbed up on the beds of the trucks to be driven to the cities, towns, or *kibbutzim* where we would spend the rest of the year. I was going to Ashdod.

I had no idea at the time that it was mentioned in the Bible. I since discovered that Ashdod was one of the major Philistine cities and that, in fact, the Ark of the Covenant ended up in Ashdod because the Philistines captured it and put it in the temple of their god Dagon right next to the god Dagon. The next day, the people of Ashdod found that Dagon had been knocked over. The Philistines kept trying subsequent days, with similar results, until finally they found Dagon with his head and limbs cut off. Then, worse. The people of Ashdod were covered with tumors, and the Philistines couldn't wait to get the Ark out of there (1 Samuel 5:1–7).

But I knew none of this when the tender let us off in front of our apartment. All I knew at the time was that my apartment was a five-minute walk to the beautiful Mediterranean Sea.

The six of us quickly found that our monthly $300 stipend for our volunteer jobs did not stretch very far, so we ate sparsely, the bulk of the money going to rent. My parents occasionally sent me money while they were supporting my brother who was still in high school. A fellow Sherut La'amnik and I shared an apartment that had recently been vacated by Moroccan Jews who apparently loved color. Every wall of every room was a different vibrant hue. Sherry and I each had a bedroom, and there was a kitchen, a living room, and a bathroom. In the bathroom was a toilet beside which was a shower with nothing separating it from the rest of the room. There was just a water sprinkler affixed to the ceiling. When we took showers, water would spray onto the floor, and subsequently into the hall.

Outside our living area was a balcony from which we were able to look out and see the sand and the road that led down to the Sea. We had very nice neighbors from Tangiers. Almost all of Ashdod was inhabited by Sephardic, or eastern Jews who came from India, Kurdistan, Iraq, Iran, Morocco, and Algiers who, because of the level of persecution in those lands against Jews, came into Israel with only what they could carry, regardless of what their social status had been in their home countries.

Apartment life was nothing like *kibbutz* life. We cooked for ourselves and washed our own clothes. I had the floor washing down pat because of the time spent on the *kibbutz*, but clothes washing? I had never washed clothes by hand. However, I knew the logistics of the washing machine, so I put all my clothes into the kitchen sink and stirred them with a large spoon. Then I squeezed them out and hung them on the line outside to dry. The stirring technique was short-lived. I learned that good old scrubbing was what clothes needed, but what a wonder to find out that the sun is an amazing bleach. My clothes were never before or since as dazzling white as they were after hanging out in the Ashdod sun.

My primary job was teaching English at Ashdod junior and senior high schools. The first day, I set out to meet the staff and get my assignment. I learned that in order to get to the school I followed a sidewalk, then a paved street, and finally the last mile wound through the sand. I had brought shoes with me that were leather with a 2 ½" heel. Students attend school six days a week in Israel, so the mile walk to and from school six days a week for a school year sent me home at the end of the Sherut La'am experience with two metal rods for heels.

I walked into the junior high first. What I thought was just a meet and greet was actually my first day of teaching. I accepted the textbook handed me and followed the headmaster and was ushered into the classroom where thirty-eight middle students were already assembled. As I walked in, the figures in navy and royal blue all stood.

"*Shalom, Ha Morah*" (Hello, teacher).

I was stunned. I had never received this kind of respect from anyone.

"Bevakesha, shev!" My broken Hebrew for "please sit." I continued to break down the respect they had been taught by insisting that they not stand for me, that we were all equal. Soon I had daily chaos. They took advantage of my very limited Hebrew. I had studied four months on *ulpan*, but remember my report card? We certainly weren't told how to say, "Stop throwing pencils" or "No hitting each other." There was a reason I was in Ashdod. What happened later came to light to me as I studied the Word and my behavior.

"Please, turn the lights back on." I looked toward a student who knew a little English and asked for the Hebrew translation. When he told me how to say it I raised my voice over the din and shouted the words I had been told. A short silence then roaring laughter! I had been told to say something filthy.

Fingerpointer

Victory begins by exposing the enemy for who he is. Satan is a mocker. From day one, he sets us up to feel humiliated, reduced, with the purpose of making us give up in embarrassment, not to pursue and accomplish our goals. Here, he used a student to make me look foolish.

I could have quit, gotten angry, retaliated. But I didn't.

Something inside us rises to overcome the mocker, the accuser. The strength of the Lord rises up, waiting.

***Do not be overcome by evil, but overcome evil with good* (Romans 12:21 NASB).**

We settled into a routine and, despite the rocky start, they learned. My teacher's book presented a simple and effective method of teaching English as a foreign language. Pronunciation for them was a challenge because in Hebrew there is no such thing as a silent consonant. So they sounded the *l*'s in *walk* and *talk*. Similar words were confused, so they cooked their food in the chicken instead of the kitchen.

That was easily remedied, but there was another letter combination that brought of gales of laughter.

"Put your tongue between your teeth like I am." I made the tongue and teeth position for the "th" combination. Astonished looks, then snickers.

"Now listen. I am going to use my voice while I say these letters in the word *this*." Loud laughter and a few hands smacking their own foreheads.

"Now watch and listen for the difference. I am going to blow out the breath, but I won't add any voice. *Thing*." Some snorting accompanied the snickers.

"Okay, your turn. Stick your tongue out between your teeth and say 'th.'" I vocalized while releasing the air. Now bodies flopped out of chairs accompanied by ribald laughter.

I raised my voice above the roar. "Now 'th,'" blowing out the air with no vocalization. Knees raised to chests and bodies rocked in hilarity on the floor.

I managed to get them back into their seats. Sheepishly they stuck their tongues between their teeth and practiced saying "this" and "thing," "that" and "thought." They glanced around to make sure no one was looking but they did practice. They learned! I started to get the teaching bug. They learned!

Footprints

The Lord watches, guides, directs. He loves us so much!

Even when we aren't thinking of Him, even when we are feeling defeated, He is right there to pick us up though we don't feel His hands. I was teaching in another country.

I didn't know the language. The students lived in hardened communities. They had fled terrorism and were hard to reach, but God, the ultimate reacher, stretched His arms around me and loved those students.

Beloved, if God so loved us, we ought also to love one another.

No man hath seen God at any time. If we love one another, God dwelleth in us, and his love is perfected in us. Hereby know we that we dwell in him, and he in us, because he hath given us of his Spirit (1 John 4:11–13 KJV).

They learned so well they were able to write little paragraphs. I began to feel the satisfaction of teaching, although I had sworn I would never in life be a teacher.

I didn't want to be a teacher. The footprints of God gently, relentlessly, override our "I wants" to become what He wants for us. *"For I know the plans I have for you," declares the LORD, "plans to prosper you and not to harm you, plans to give you hope and a future"* (Jeremiah 29:11 NIV).

But here was this conglomeration of students, whose first language was Arabic, French, or Farsi, learning English because I was teaching them. It was exhilarating. Why was their first language not Hebrew? None of the students had Hebrew as a first language because none of them were Sabras, Israeli born. The settlement town of Ashdod was only ten years old, so none of them was born there. As I immersed myself in Hebrew day after day, I learned what sloppy speakers we Americans are, sounding as if we are speaking with marbles in our mouths.

In the morning I had the junior high, and in the afternoon the senior high. These senior high school students were lovely. They already had some knowledge of English, so we were able to concentrate on writing essays and having intelligent conversation. As tensions mounted in the months before the Six Day War, I gave them assignments to write about their feelings concerning the situation. It was fascinating to learn about their lives and beliefs. Afternoons at the high school were breaths of fresh air after my mornings in the tumultuous junior high. I taught night classes, too. These were adults who worked during the day, and they were delightful. They came by choice, and I think our class was an opportunity to make friends as well as to learn English.

My days started to take on a rhythm. Six days a week I got up, walked to the grocer to pick up one of the warm loaves of bread that were stacked unwrapped on the floor beneath the window, took it back to the apartment, and ate the bread with sweet butter and an egg that was fresh and delicious. Then I got into my dress and heels and walked the two miles to the junior high school.

Chapter Seventeen

Building Trust in the Moadone Gangs

By far, the most challenging assignment I was given was the *moadone* (club). My job description was to help immigrant youth and teens become acclimated to life in Israel by spending time with them after school in a club and involving them in activities that would foster cooperation. I would get home from school, have a quick supper of the scant food we were able to afford, change clothes into something more casual, and head for the walk down the highway a couple of miles to a large cement building.

I felt like a complete fraud. Here I was, an American going back to a home in the USA, telling a group of tormented teens, who had been ripped from their homelands because their own countrymen hated them, that they should get acclimated to this new land. How quickly I was maturing. My mind had been on Euchre games, tricycle races, and now I was identifying with the torment of my teenage immigrants, whom I grew so to love.

The young people in the *moadone*, like the students I taught, were from North African countries like Tunisia, Tangiers, Algiers; and Middle Eastern countries like Egypt, Yemen, Iran, Iraq, and Kurdistan. They were hated in their countries, and their lives had been in danger daily because they were Jews. The Jewish Agency helped them to immigrate to Israel. Their parents felt betrayed. They had been shown brochures about the Promised Land. They had assumed they would be able to have homes and jobs similar to the ones they left, if not better. They came to Israel with only what they could carry, with no Hebrew and no Israeli certification for their professions, so the majority was reduced from a socioeconomic group that held respect and prosperity to the bottom rung, to menial labor or no work at all.

Yes, these poor, angry youth living in crowded poverty were Jews. The two bedroom apartments into which the Jewish Agency put the immigrants held perhaps ten people. Many had left businesses and come to Israel to find themselves living in squalor. With the overcrowding and lack of adequate employment, tempers flared. Products of those homes were the youth who were in my *moadone*.

Fingerpointer

Perhaps fathers had threatened their children not to say a word about the violence that was in the homes, violence that was fueled by their frustration.

Or perhaps the children just had a family loyalty.

In every culture, it seems that children act out in public what parents intend to keep secret. Children's behaviors seem to be wide screens broadcasting the tangled wires of their homes. These young people came, furious, to *my moadone.*

Hatred and threats. That is the language of the enemy of our souls. Satan hates and destroys. It is horrifying when a human being cooperates with the tormentor.

Here we have the layered lie: Satan tells the fathers that they are nothing because they can no longer earn money. Satan tells the fathers to take it out on their children.

Satan tells the children to fear the abusive parent. All lies. Our fight of faith is to refuse to believe in or cooperate with the father of lies.

"You are of your father the devil, and your will is to do your father's desires. He was a murderer from the beginning, and does not stand in

the truth, because there is no truth in him. When he lies, he speaks out of his own character, for he is a liar and the father of lies **(John 8:44 ESV).**

They were ready to fight, to rebel, to do anything except what was expected of them. This wasn't school. There were no grades, no incentive to behave or produce.

This was Satan at work.

I walked into chaos that first day. The three-story, cement building was divided into large rooms, each packed with youth and teens who had been divided by age. Some of the rooms had no windows, and the young men took twisted pleasure in turning off the lights and hurling chairs through the pitch-blackness. Amazingly, no one was hurt. The third floor room did have a window, and the older boys created a game. They would line up on both sides of the window. Then one of the boys would run, full speed, down the middle of the rows, and when he reached the window, the boys closest would throw him out the window to the cement three stories below. Noise! Pandemonium! Blood. Yes, blood. The police were frequently at the bottom of that window.

Footprints

Chaos. God is a God of order. He took the chaos and created order. There is something in us—who are made in His image—that wants order.

We organize, straighten, design for order. Satan is the author of the chaotic. Imagine the thrill he got out of watching the blood, the pain, and my fear.

For God is not a God of disorder but of peace (1 Corinthians 14:33 NIV).

This mass of anger and frustration faced me day after day. What to do? I had to reach them somehow. I had to gain their trust.

"Don't let your hearts be troubled. Trust in God, and trust also in me" (John 14:1 NLT).

At the time, I didn't know to ask the Holy Spirit for help, for guidance. I had grown up on the Old Testament:

"Hear O Israel: The LORD our God, the LORD is one!" (Deuteronomy 6:4 NKJV).

I don't recall ever learning anything about the need to trust people, only God.

But I knew that if I were to have these kids' hearts I had to build their trust in me. They needed me, even if they didn't know it.

I took a risk and picked the meanest, the biggest troublemaker in the older group, a youth from Morocco, and asked him to do me a favor. I gave him the equivalent of a $20.00 bill and asked him to go to the local cinema and buy me one movie ticket, which would be like $1.00 and bring me the change. He *flew* down the steps and out the door, sand scuffling up behind his sandaled feet. After about twenty minutes he was back, beaming!

In one hand he held a ticket, and in the other hand he held all the change. In that proud moment, he became my helper, my protector, my crowd controller, my dear friend. Much later, I learned in Acts 22:4–15 that enemies don't have to remain so, but it takes revelation for eyes and heart to open to truth. In my case the eyes and heart that were opened were mine. I had to *see* into the depths of these tormented youth to be able to discern the problem, and I had to survey the contents of my own heart to remove the fear and fill it with faith.

Fear would have crippled me. I had to see I had the power to find a solution, and I had the love necessary to break down walls, and I had the soundness of mind to carry the plan out.

Footprints

Perfect love casts out fear. Love was in my heart for those kids because God put it there. Love had to cast out the fear or I couldn't win their trust.

There is no fear in love. But perfect love drives out fear, because fear has to do with punishment. The one who fears is not made perfect in love (1 John 4:18 NIV).

Oh! Courage, soundness of mind, and power to move in with the necessary plan, has stood me all these years in ministry. I needed no protection and no control after that. From that day on, everything changed. We became a family. I even invited them to my apartment and listened to stories of their lives in Morocco, Tangiers, Algeria, Yeman, or Iraq.

What a privilege to live in Israel, the country closest to God's heart. Once I stepped on the soil, I was no longer Cheryl, the silly, foolish trivial girl. I was a woman. I was a woman of the Land.

Every night, I walked home alone from the *moadone* in pitch black. There were no streetlights along the highway and no cars. It was impossible to see even a few feet in front of me. One night I tripped over something that had been strung across the road. I couldn't see what it was, but I felt my flesh tear. I kept walking until I got home and saw that my shin had been ripped open by barbed wire. The next morning, at the first sign of sun, I hurried to the medical clinic where everyone would come and take a number. I was already number 71.

I waited in the hallway where all up and down were specimens of pain and suffering. Old men were slumped against the walls, pitiful women were sitting on benches, some held up by others. Elderly sufferers lay on the floor some with huge cataracts hanging out of their eyes. Misery.

My turn to go in. I showed my leg.

"Here is your first shot. You will come back tomorrow."

"For what?"

"For the next shot. You will have seven more shots."

I left and never went back for more shots. I still have the scars on my leg and kept my eyes open for barbed wire the rest of the school year on that walk to and from the *moadone*.

Chapter Eighteen

My Cousin Was Cut Up and Thrown into a Bedouin Well!

I had never hitchhiked before I went to Israel, but it became our main source of travel. We would stand at the side of the road with our arms pointed in the direction we wanted to go, the index finger pointing to the street. We would get rides mostly in tenders. I was foolish and took risks. Once, a friend and I were hitchhiking, and the driver stopped in some kind of an Arabic community with an olive grove.

"Take off your clothes," he said. "Do it!" he snapped, enraged.

We ran like mad through families of picnicking Arabs and got away from him and started on another highway.

Another time, I was hitchhiking alone and saw a car with a Mogen David Adom sticker (Red Star of David), which indicated that he was a doctor. He stopped and I went to the window. He looked my dad's age, and since he was a doctor I felt safe. I hopped into the passenger seat.

"Shalom! Atah doma abba shelee!" (Hi. You remind me of my dad!)

"Have you been to Natanya?" he asked, smiling as he merged back onto the highway.

"No."

"Well, I'll take you to meet my wife and children. Would you like that?"

"Thanks, that would be great!" An Israeli family experience in a town I'd never visited. We drove up to an apartment, and he took me to the door and opened it. The smell was that of a place left vacant for months. There was so sign of life.

"Where is everyone?"

"Oh they are visiting my wife's family. How about taking a shower? You can go in there." He pointed to a door. "I won't look." I scanned the apartment and noticed a room with a dentist's chair. Thinking quickly:

"What's that?"

"I am a dentist. I have my office in my home."

"Hey! How about checking my teeth? I haven't had my teeth checked in months." I scampered up on the chair and opened my mouth. He stared for a minute, then got out his dental tools and looked in my mouth.

"Your teeth are fine. You have beautiful eyes. Now get down. I'm taking you back to the highway. Be careful and stop hitchhiking. It's dangerous."

He took me to the road. I got out, and he drove back the way he had come. Did he have a twinge of conscience, or was he trying to teach me a lesson?

I did not stop hitchhiking, though. I continued doing it all during my stay in Israel, sometimes in groups, sometime in pairs, and often alone. Everywhere we went, we were admonished by people who, amazingly enough, all had the same cousin. "Shula, don't hitchhike! My cousin's body was found cut up in the bottom of a Bedouin well."

Footprints

So many things I did were stupid and unnecessarily risky.

I could have easily been raped or killed. Don't do these things, young reader.

But looking back, even though I did not deserve it, I see the protection of the Father on His child. I put Him through so much trouble. He spent so much time protecting me. The Word says He never sleeps but watches over us.

Behold, He who keeps Israel will neither slumber nor sleep.

The LORD is your keeper; the LORD is your shade on your right hand.

The sun will not smite you by day, nor the moon by night (Psalm 121:4–6 NASB).

Grocery shopping, of course, was done on foot. I would grab my string bag and head out to various shops. There was the green grocer who sold fruits and vegetables. All the lovely produce was sent out of the country, so little Ashdod was left with bruised fruits and wilted vegetables. The butcher shop sold chickens hanging by their feet and slabs of beef attacked by bombing flies in the hot Israeli sun. I still remember the price of the ground beef because it was what I bought when I could afford it. It was the equivalent of $12.00 a pound.

When it got cold in the winter, and it did, we had a space heater, which we also used as a toaster by turning it on its side and placing bread on the slats. In Israel, in those days, people didn't have cats as pets. Cats were wild, like squirrels. They even looked different from our cats. Their bodies were long and lean with wide eyes that took up most of their narrow faces. But I found a cat and made it a pet. We called him *Ma Pitome*, which meant, "all of a sudden," because all of a sudden there he was. He was wild inside and outside. One time we left a chicken out defrosting on the counter while we were at work. We came home to cook and found that Ma Pitome had flung the chicken onto the floor, chowed down on it, and that was the end of dinner.

One afternoon, my roommate and I were in the apartment and there was a knock on the door.

"May I come in and show you something that you cannot live without?"

Never before or since did we have a salesman come to our door in Israel. We ushered him in and invited him to sit at the small table where we shared meals. There he spread out three thick volumes of *The Complete English-Hebrew and the Complete Hebrew-English Dictionary* by Reuben Alcalay (Massadah Publishing Company, Tel-Aviv-Jerusalem. 1962, 1965).

"Imagine how this will improve your Hebrew!" he exclaimed, opening the volumes so that we could see the pages.

"Sure! How much?" I loved any opportunity to improve my Hebrew.

"I'll tell you what," he said. "You keep the books. Pay me part now, and the first of the next three months I will come by to get the rest until it's paid. "

Sherry and I devoured the dictionaries. First there was the Hebrew word, then the English translation followed by phrases to illuminate the meaning. Every evening we would take turns reading Hebrew words, definitions and phrases:

Hebrew: *azav*. English: leave, leave behind, quit, loosen, release, relinquish, set free, let go; to omit.

We had no television or phone; there was no library or bookstore so our Hebrew-English dictionary was our evening pastime. We read and read and read Hebrew words and English definitions with illuminating phrases.

Footprints

Illuminating phrases: *azav: "Therefore shall a man leave his father and mother and shall cleave (cling) to his wife, so that they become one Flesh"* (Genesis 2:24).

My God, my God, why have You forsaken me? (Psalm 22:1 KJV).

Never stop studying! If you forsake study for one day, it will forsake you for two.

Little did I know that September 29, 1983, I would begin teaching a thirty-year study on the book of Psalms, two verses at a time beginning with Psalm 1:1–2, dissecting each with an in-depth study by reading the Hebrew, then the English, and illuminating them with phrases. Who knew? Who *could* know? I had never read the Bible. I had no desire to read the Bible. But we devoured the Hebrew dictionary. Hebrew became a foundational part of my teaching from the book of Psalms. I extracted significant words from the Scripture, find the Hebrew by looking in a concordance, and then pull down my Hebrew-English dictionary that I bought in Ashdod.

Occasionally, there would be visits from Sherut La'amniks stationed elsewhere in Israel, and sometimes we would visit them by bus or by hitching rides on the highway. One time, we had so many guests from other Sherut La'amniks that there were twenty people eating the evening meal. The one kilo of ground beef amazingly stretched to feed us all. When dinner was over and night fell, there was no way the guests could leave. The buses didn't run on Shabbat. So out came blankets and sleeping bags, and our guests spent the night.

I had never read the New Testament, and the group of us around the table was not devout. Later, when I read the story of Jesus multiplying the boy's lunch in every one of the gospels, I remembered how God multiplied that kilo of ground beef.

Another time, a friend and I had gone out of town, but Shabbat came, and we found that there was no place to eat. No busses to get home. We sat on the curb and put our faces in our hands. We must have looked pitiful because two lovely women approached us.

"Ma yesh?" (What's wrong?) We explained that we were so hungry and there were no restaurants or shops open. The two ladies whispered for a few seconds then signaled for us to follow. They took us home and gave us thickly sliced bread slathered with the most delicious butter and chunky preserves ever to touch our mouths. I never forgot that act of kindness, taking us into her home, and feeding us. It became a foundational piece of Women with a Vision: Showing Hospitality through Sharing Food.

In March, I hitchhiked to visit Shoshana, who was a teacher on a *kibbutz* right below the Golan Heights. She showed me around and told me about nights.

"The children can't sleep in their houses because the Syrians shoot at the children's houses every night. We have to make them beds in the bomb shelters." She led me to the bomb shelters and, sure enough, I leaned over and saw little beds and shelves.

"Teaching here is so different than teaching in the USA.," Shoshana said as we walked the grounds of the *kibbutz*. "We can use no form of competition. None! No one student can think he did better than others. No one wins. No one loses. The emphasis is on team, on community. If they don't want to come to class, they sleep in. It's been tough to get used to." Shoshana had been a teacher in the United States, and this was a far cry from the classroom of the individual and from encouraging each student to be the best. It is interesting to know that despite lack of competition, of prodding to do their best, many of Israel's political and military leaders in the 1950s and 60s came from *kibbutz* movement.

Chapter Nineteen
Did I Fall in Love or off a Cliff?

One day, I met a fellow teacher at the high school. He was gorgeous, dark, and Iraqi Kurd. As dark as he was, I was light. I was slim after being sick and losing twelve pounds on the *kibbutz*. My blonde hair and green eyes contrasted with his bronze skin and black eyes. My figure was fit from the miles of walking to school on sand Sunday through Friday. Quickly, we were a couple. Before long, we were inseparable. Where there was Rafi, there was Shula. Rafi and Shula. As Rafi's little nephew put it:

"Hineh Shula shel Rafi!" (Here comes Rafi's Shula.)

The Marine? I had come alive in Israel, slithered into my new skin, and there just was no room in there anymore for the Marine.

Oh, the love! The love! The love! I adored Rafi. He would come visit me, spend hours in my apartment, and have meals with me. Why wasn't he introducing me to his family? Why wouldn't he invite me to his house? We spent every waking moment together. On weekends, we would promenade, just walk around. It was the thing that was done in Ashdod on evenings and on *Erev Shabbat* (Sabbath Eve) before the stores closed. We would walk around the *merkaz* (center) and look in the shops, greet other friends, have an iced coffee or *gleeda* (ice cream).

We were becoming more and more serious, even talking about marriage. Rafi finally invited me home to meet his family. Before sundown one *Erev Shabbat,* Rafi led me to his house. We turned off the pavement and started walking through dusty pathways past little tiny houses strewn, without apparent plan, like a patchwork of stone amid dust and sand. Continuing to wind around, we came to a small house. Rafi kissed his hand and placed it on the *Mezuzah,* which was on the doorpost, and I did the same. Mezuzah is a beautiful container for a portion of Scripture. *And thou shalt write them upon the posts of thy house and on thy gates* (Deuteronomy 6:9 KJV).

Every Jewish home that I know of has a scroll in a decorative container nailed on the doorpost. The Scriptures tell us to love God with all our hearts and tell of the blessings we will have for doing so. It is traditional to kiss it upon leaving and entering the house by putting fingers to the lips and then onto the Mezuzah.

Walking into the dimly lit room, I saw a smiling, broad-faced woman squatting on the floor. She stood up and there she was, stocky, just my height, braids down to the back of her legs past her knees, standing eye to eye with me in front of an enormous bowl, more than two feet in diameter, full of raw rice from which she had been removing impurities. She gave me a hug. She was so short that I could gaze over her shoulder and take in the room behind her. We separated, and as politely as I could, I turned in a pivot to stare at the rest of the room. In the corner was an old woman on her haunches eating out of a bowl on the floor. A man wearing a hat lay on a side bench of the room, exactly where he was every time I saw him in the months to come. He was just lying there, shooting sunflower seeds out of his mouth across the room onto the floor.

One by one, Rafi's seven siblings came out of the one adjacent room. When I went into the bathroom, I found a toilet with no seat and no paper. I didn't see a shower. Rafi later told me that all of them shared one toothbrush.

Maybe Rafi was embarrassed to take me home, but immediately I took his mama to my heart, and I could tell that she fell in love with me, as well. His little brothers and sisters were precious, and his sister-in-law and I became very close in the months to come as the nation mobilized for war and her husband, along with Rafi, left.

Surely, there was a *shul* (synagogue) in Ashdod, but I never saw one, and in fact, never heard anyone even say prayer before a meal until I met Rafi's family. They were *Dati* (Orthodox). The *Barucha* (blessing before the meal) was said—not before each meal but before each *bite*. Yes! Before each bite Rafi's father (who I discovered was a hypocrite, unless you call a wife beater a man of faith) would say the entire blessing of the bread.

Baruch atah adonai elohenu melech ha olam ha motzeh lechem min ha aretz. Blessed art Thou, O Lord our God, king of the universe, who bringeth forth the bread from the earth.

Even though their family spoke Aramaic, as did all the Iraqis in Kurdistan, the prayers, as they are with Jews worldwide, were spoken in Hebrew.

I ended up sharing many meals in Rafi's home. His mother spent hours and hours in the kitchen dicing tomatoes, washing rice, cleaning beans. I loved helping her. Breakfast always included a cup of hot coffee or tea because Rafi's mom said that without something hot in the morning you get headaches. Eggs were always prepared like this: *Eema* (mama) poured about three tablespoons of oil into a pan and heated it. She cracked three eggs into a bowl and added ½ cup of water and ¼ cup of flour. She beat the mixture and dropped it into the hot oil producing a poof-y golden brown pillow of egg that was substantial because of the added flour. For supper we often had a huge bowl of green beans topped with maybe a one-inch square of fatty beef.

Pesach (Passover) was the best! In addition to the traditional service of reading about the children of Israel leaving bondage in Egypt to freedom, there was a game afterwards. A huge bowl of hardboiled eggs was placed in the middle of the table. Everyone in the family took one. Rafi had seven brothers and sisters, and one brother was married, so there was a crowd around the table. The goal of the game was to smash each other's eggs, and the one whose egg remained uncracked was the winner.

Eema's specialty from her country was *kubbeh. Kubbeh* were dumplings made of semolina flour, ideally with delicious vegetables and meat inside. But the family was so poor and with so many mouths, including mine, Eema made a big, fat round ball—the shape and look of a very large matzo ball—formed around at most ½ tablespoon of fatty meat mixture. The food took its toll on me, and either from that or something else, I became really sick from both ends and ended up in bed unable to do anything but groan. Eema offered to send over some *kubbeh*, but I declined gracefully. The family cure for diarrhea was to drink rice water, and that did work. She boiled a small amount of rice for me in a pot of water, strained it, cooled it, and gave me the water to drink. In no time it took effect.

In the evenings, Eema and I often sat in the living room, which would be transformed into a bedroom at night by opening bedrolls. She shared her life with me, what it was like living back in Kurdistan.

She shared, looking far beyond my face, that she was married before she had her period. She made a fist and shot it toward her face to let me know that her husband beat her. Her eyes held such pain. But her face brightened a little when she spoke about the past. In the Hebrew that she could barely speak, and I could by now understand, she told me about the opulent lifestyle they had. "Every window was a different color. We had swans on our lake." She spread her hands, palms upward, to indicate that they had everything anyone would need. "But they were killing Jews, hanging them in the square or beheading them and posting their heads on fences. Then, they finally forced all the Jews out of Kurdistan. We had to leave and take our children to safety. We could bring only what we could carry." She lifted a hand on each side of her waist to indicate the bags she had brought.

In Ashdod, Rafi's dad did open a little store, but it was nothing like what they left back home. She reached across and patted my knee. Her stomach was hugely swollen and she often groaned quietly of pain. I just hugged her, not knowing how else to help.

Footprints

The tiny embryo of the mercy gift was just starting to form in me as I sat with the dear mother of the man from whom I was becoming inseparable. I loved this sweet mama whose pain I could only comfort with hugs and sighs.

I have so many visual memories of Ashdod. Children fishing with their hands for small fish that swam close to the shore. A small Indian boy sitting on the sandy sidewalk, his shadow behind him. The beautiful sea. The beach covered with shells, which would become our *Menorah* (candelabra) as *Chanukah* (Festival of Lights) approached. We gathered nine shells and placed candles in them, one for each of the eight nights of Chanukah, and the center for the Shamash or servant candle. The markets were not the colorful markets presented in travel programs on television. No. These markets were built of makeshift planks with rotting chickens hanging by their feet and slabs of beef out in the hot sun, flies hovering, with scanty vegetables and fruits. The *merkaz* (center) featured youths strolling slowly to see and be seen. There were guys with shirts open to the middle of their chests and girls in their party best. Rafi and I always were part of the promenade.

"See how beautiful is Shula, even without makeup?" he would brag, smiling.

Most of the Ashdod girls wore lots of dark kohl around their eyes. Rafi had a group of male friends, and it was with them that I spent time if not with his family. I had separated myself from the other *Sherut La'amniks* in Ashdod and immersed myself in the local culture and language. For that reason, I was fluent in Hebrew in the few months that I was in Ashdod.

Ashdod had five stores and two restaurants.

My favorite restaurant was on a corner, owned by a woman whom I called the Hungarian Romanian lady because she told us her background which included those two countries. She made the best food! My favorite was her soup. I don't know how she cut those vegetables so very tiny—miniscule, smaller than anything produced by the "as seen on TV" gadgets sold in the states today. Oh, that soup was thick with those vegetables almost shredded. And her *schnitzel*—oh, the taste! And her pastries. I don't like rum, but her rum cakes were moist and fairly dripped of honey and rum. And the cheese roll. Nothing like it anywhere. Fluffy dough with a dollop, no a mound, no a pillow of rich cheeses the likes of which I have never tasted before or since, the flaky crust kissing its contents.

The other restaurant was gourmet and elite—for whom I don't know because I didn't know anyone who even had a telephone or an automobile, never mind lots of money to spend on extravagant meals. But twice we went. Special occasions.

"*Shalom! Shalom!* Can you go and get your friends?" The owner begged us to leave and bring others in. We could not have called them because the restaurant didn't have a phone. The only dish I remember at the fancy, expensive restaurant was a rich tomato soup with strands of melting cheese.

But the Hungarian-Romanian lady's homelike cooking—now I want to take two fingers, hold them to my mouth, kiss them, and throw that kiss your way! Oh, it was delicious!

I had never observed dietary laws in the states, and there surely were none on the nonreligious *kibbutz*. But in Ashdod they were strict about milk and meat. Observant (Orthodox) Jews do not mix milk and meat because of the Scripture: *"You shall not boil a young goat in its mother's milk"* (Deuteronomy 14:21 NKJV). From that came the division of milk and meat, the elaborate kitchen with milk dishes, pots, pans, silverware, and another set of each for meat; in some, another set for Pesach (Passover). I have even known some observant American Jews who have two ovens and two dishwashers so that no dish would ever hold meat one day and milk another.

Being a Reform Jew, I was used to enjoying a cup of coffee with cream and sugar after meals. No way, not in Ashdod. According to the Jewish law of *Kashruth* (keeping kosher, also part of the Levitical law), after eating meat one had to wait six hours to have dairy. We American *Sherut La'amniks* would sometimes wheedle and cajole our Hungarian-Romanian lady, and once or twice, out of annoyance, having been beaten down with our spoiled American whining, she would give a sharp nod of her head toward the adjacent room of the restaurant and we got the hint. We scampered over there and sat at a table while she reluctantly brought us coffee with cream, barely looking at us as she set it down.

Once, totally forgetting the law of *Kashruth*, I grabbed a few candy bars on the way to Rafi's house to give to his younger brothers and sisters. But, because they had just eaten dinner, they had to wait *six hours* to eat their chocolate bars. I felt so bad seeing their little faces unable to enjoy their rare treats until morning because dinner was at six—they would have to wait until midnight for their chocolate bars. I never made that mistake again.

Rafi and I were constantly together, so when it was time for the annual Four Day March, he asked me to go with him and his team from the high school. *Oy!* What in the world was I in for? Yes, I was used to walking miles per week over sand, but I was no match for this. We started at three in the morning and walked until noon. My legs. Never have I felt such pain. Not my feet. It was my legs.

There were tents everywhere as we prepared for the night. For toilets, ditches were dug and boards put across for hundreds of marchers. Food was cold corn and beans out of cans. The next day and the subsequent three days, I rode in one of the trucks provided for softies like me who couldn't make the rest of the trek on foot.

When we got back from the four-day march, Rafi told me that he expected me to be sexually intimate with him, but I refused. He told me then he would find any of the Israeli girls because they all had sex with their boyfriends. I was so stupid I believed him, and because I didn't want to be lonely, I gave in. It wasn't long before I missed my period.

Chapter Twenty

There Are None Good, No Not One

I thought of a conversation I had two months before in the apartment of one of the Ashdod volunteers. We were having coffee, talking about life back in the USA.

"I got a letter from my friend back in the States," said Lynne. "She got pregnant with some guy she barely knew and wrote me that she got an abortion."

"Abortion!" I had sputtered out. "How can she even *live* with herself after that?" All eyes had turned onto my self-righteous face, and then they went on talking about jobs back home, classes, and boyfriends left behind.

So now, two months later, I was sitting with Rafi in my apartment. My roommate was gone, and the silence was roaring in my ears.

"Rafi," I told him in Hebrew. "I think I'm pregnant."

Fingerpointer

Satan had set me up. He had told me about the girl having the abortion, nudged me to judge her, and then led me into sin so I would be in the same situation. I was filled with guilt at myself, at my own weakness, and with the echo in my ears of my judgmental words against her.

Then I heard a loud voice in heaven say, "Now have come the salvation and the power and the kingdom of our God, and the authority

of his Messiah. For the accuser of our brothers and sisters, who accuses them before our God day and night, has been hurled down" (Revelation 12:10 NIV).

How wonderful that one day we will no longer have to deal with the accuser.

His reply was swift. "You will find out, and you will have an abortion."

I was horrified. Never! "No! I will not have an abortion. You will marry me!"

But no. Rafi's plan was that he would save the money, come to the States, and we would marry in Michigan City, Indiana, in my synagogue. But in the meantime, Rafii assured me that all the girls had abortions in Israel and that I would, too.

I was so weak, so stupid. Had I forgotten that he had said *all* the girls in Ashdod were having sex with their boyfriends? I cried. I begged. I patted my stomach.

That *Erev Shabbat,* we were walking in the *merkaz* like we did every *Erev Shabbat.* We passed a store window with a reflection, and I cradled my tummy.

Fingerpointer

"Stop that!" Rafi hissed. "People will see."

See how stupid you were! The voice of the mocker seemed to sneer.

Later, I discovered a Scripture that says, "Out in the open wisdom calls aloud, she raises her voice in the public square" (Proverbs 1:20 NIV).

We can always know the right thing to do because wisdom speaks. The question is, are we listening?

I went to the clinic alone, and in Hebrew told the doctor, *"Yeshlee teenooket b' betin"* (I have a baby in my belly). The doctor examined me and took a test and confirmed it. He saw my face and his own broke with sorrow.

Footprints

Father God showed me, through the broken look on that doctor's face, that I was killing a precious child and breaking the Lord's heart.

Jesus said, "Let the little children come to me, and do not hinder them, for the kingdom of heaven belongs to such as these" (Matthew 19:14 NIV).

"You don't want it?"

God is so gentle. He shows us ourselves using the Word. As we are judging people in the scenario, He gives us a little nudge and a mirror so that we can see ourselves.

"Do not judge so that you will not be judged. For in the way you judge, you will be judged; and by your standard of measure, it will be measured to you" (Matthew 7:1–2 NASB).

I shook my head, tears running down my face. He looked at me, his eyes soft as if they were looking at his own granddaughter whose heart was breaking. Yes, I did want it! It was my baby. It was our baby. But Rafi wouldn't marry me, and I didn't want to disgrace my family. I so wanted to make my parents proud. It seemed I was never able to do anything that made them proud. I would snap at my mother when she told me what dazzling things other young women were doing. I felt as if she were rubbing my nose in the fact that while they were conquering the world, I was doing nothing. So, finally, I had an opportunity to make them proud, going to serve with *Sherut La'am for* a year. My desire to make them proud would be blown to splinters if I told them I was pregnant.

Fingerpointer

They saved up the money to send you here and what do you do with it? *You kill their grandchild!*

Sure, go home pregnant, and then what will the community think of your parents, the daughter they raised?

Satan is a master at slapping us first on one cheek then on the other, bombarding us with accusations and taunts. Satan distorts the Word to use it against us.

Be wise, my [daughter], and make my heart glad, that I may reply to him that reproaches me (Proverbs 27:11 NASB).

Instead of being the gentle footprint of the Lord teaching or guiding me, this was Satan using the same Scripture to leave me with no hope.

"I have humiliated my parents, and they would be the reproach of everyone if my sin was obvious, as it would be in the presence of a new baby." Satan was also showing me that I was killing a baby and I couldn't be forgiven because God loved the baby.

All of my concerns about going home pregnant had to do with pride. I wouldn't be seen as the girl I wanted to pretend to be. My parents would be the laughingstock because of me.

When pride comes then comes disgrace, but with the humble is wisdom (Proverbs 11:2 ESV).

If I only had the courage to go home pregnant with my baby.

My dear parents had continually sacrificed to send me gifts and money at the same time they were saving for Jeff's college. They had the whole college thing planned perfectly. I would graduate one year, and Jeff would start the following fall. But the year in Israel, agreed to by my parents out of a desperate move to get me away from one awful relationship, would force them to have double payments when I returned to the USA.

I don't recall Rafi ever paying for anything—meals, gifts, nothing. I paid for everything and even bought things for everyone in his family on many occasions. And now I was planning to use love-money sent by my precious parents to kill their grandchild.

We took off work and walked to the abortion clinic on a Monday, early afternoon.

Ashdod was the site of the god Dagon—the one God had overthrown and crumbled thousands of years before. Now here I was, participating in the ancient rite of infant sacrifice. Never having read the Bible, I did not learn the magnitude of what I had done and the significance of it in that particular setting until fifteen years later when I was reading through the Bible and came to 1 Samuel 5. I stopped breathing when I read about Ashdod being the place where the god Dagon stood. I had killed my baby in the same place. I learned that the primary way Dagon's cult followers worshiped him was through the human sacrifice . . . of babies.

But, at that time, I didn't know anything except that I was pregnant, and in an hour the whole thing would be over. I would no longer be pregnant, so I wouldn't have to embarrass my parents. It would be over. Over. Over.

"Can Rafi come in with me?" I asked,

The nurse looked at me horrified.

"Oh! No! We can't even stand watching these. We wouldn't ever ask anyone else to watch it!"

Footprints

The Lord continued to show me how much He hated abortion by letting me see how horrifying it was to people who had to view it.

As I lay on that table having a legal abortion in Israel, it was still illegal in the USA.

But in 1973, Roe v. Wade would make it legal. Suddenly, it was not the murder of children. It was the woman's right to choose. But I held the look of that nurse's face in my heart and her words in my ears to know the truth of abortion. "Oh, no! We can't even stand watching these. Oh no. We can't even stand watching these. Oh, no. We can't even stand watching these." And the sorrowful face of the precious doctor who mirrored my tear-streaked face, "You don't want it?"

In today's society with the big rift between secular and religious thinking—with pro-life and pro-choice—we get the idea that those who perform abortions think they are doing a service to society, a favor for women. Yet, right there in that abortion clinic where there was not an empty seat in the room of waiting girls, the words echoed in my head—and echo now, still.

"Would you like anesthetic? It is for people who are nervous. There is an extra cost." The nurse was talking to me, but I was still thinking about those words, "We can't stand watching them."

I hesitated.

Rafi spoke up, "Shula doesn't need anesthetic."

I looked at the nurse.

"I am very nervous. I do." I am so aware now of how unfeeling Rafi was for me—never paying for anything, telling the nurse I didn't need an anesthetic. But, I was either in love or I had fallen off a cliff into darkness.

I lay down on the table, the nurse gave me an IV, and I remember nothing. It was over. I was so relieved. I got away with it. No one would ever know. It lasted thirty minutes, and it was over. Or, so I thought. Actually, it was a procedure that has lasted up to this moment. Even now, forty-eight years later, I am—in my heart and mind—still a mother who murdered her infant. It was at that instant that I realized I had broken all of the Ten Commandments. Mr. Goldman, my religious teacher at Sinai Temple had us memorize them—not the short version. We memorized and recited every word of Exodus 20:1–17, and now they were playing before my face. I didn't have to look them up or strain to remember. They were written on my heart.

1. I was not making God the center of my life.
2. There were mountains of things that filled my mind more than God did.
3. I took His name in vain.
4. I did not honor the Sabbath day or keep it holy.
5. I didn't honor my mother and father. I had taken the money they had scrimped to send me and murdered their grandchild.
6. I did steal. The Marine, the man my parents couldn't get me away from fast enough, had influenced me to steal a few small items for the risk of it.
7. I was fornicating. It wasn't adultery, but it was just as bad.
8. I murdered.
9. And I was jealous of anyone who made their parents proud of them.
10. I did bear false witness against that upstanding young man who lied for me.

I tried to put all this out of my mind for the next decades. But I was obsessed. I was obsessed with fetuses, with embryos. If I heard of a girl who got pregnant out of wedlock and kept her babies, I didn't see her as promiscuous, I saw her as a heroine, a saint.

I was too ashamed to go home pregnant. For that, I take full responsibility. I could have insisted. It was my body. I could have said, "This is my child, and no one can rip it out of me." But I did not. Instead I took the coward's way out.

When I woke up, I was in a recliner in a family room where a teenager, most likely the son, was sitting at a table doing homework. He smiled at me shyly. Rafi helped me out of the chair and walked me over two miles of sand, bleeding. Back in my apartment, I lay weak, until I gathered enough strength to go back to work.

I had remained friends with the city family that I used to visit every weekend, but I saw them only once in a while after I recognized the father's advances toward me. His mother did not at all approve of Rafi. He was a Sephardic Jew, not Ashkenazi. In Israel there was a huge class distinction between the two. Ashkenazi Jews were from Eastern Europe, and Sephardic Jews were from Spain, Portugal, the Middle East, and North Africa. In Israel, Sephardic Jews seemed to be in a considerably lower socioeconomic level. For that reason, Israel took care to find the best and brightest among the Sephardic Jews and educate them so that they could raise the socioeconomic level among that population through education. When I told Pera that Rafi was going to college, she scoffed.

"Those people are like gold," she had spat. She knew he hadn't taken *bagrut,* (prerequisite examination for higher education). "If he even showed a glimmer of promise, they would be snapping him up to get him ready to send to university. Why are you throwing your life away for someone like him? Your parents didn't send you here to end up with a Sephardic."

I am embarrassed to show the discrimination against Sephardic Jews, but I'm showing Israel as I experienced it in 1966–67. She had no idea that I had an abortion.

A couple of months after I had the abortion, I ran into them again in Tel Aviv.

"Shula! Shula! Look at you! You came to us plump and now you are skinny like a cat. Your mother will not recognize you."

Chapter Twenty-One
To Die for Israel Is to Die for God

It was May 1967. The talks of impending war in Israel made it into the international news, and my parents sent me special delivery letters.

"Cheryl, come home."

Then, "Cheryl, for Daddy's sake, come home."

Then one from Sinai Temple, "Cheryl, please return home."

I refused to leave. The *Sachnut* (Jewish Agency) came to our door and told my roommate and me that it was time to evacuate Americans. I told him I would think about it. My idea of war was World War II, which lasted years, and Vietnam, which lasted decades. I assumed that I would be able to help with bandages and clinics. I made my decision.

The next day, the man from *Sachnut* returned. "No. I'm going to stay. To die for Israel is to die for God." Yes, I did believe that. For me to die for Israel *was* to die for God. The two were intertwined in my mind. God. Israel. I loved Israel so much. I felt one with it.

A couple of months earlier, I had been speaking with the family with whom I was spending weekends. I said, "Israel is our country and I'm so proud of it."

The son piped up, "It's not your country." The mother shushed him.

But it was. Israel was my country, and defending it would be defending what mattered to God.

I found out later that my parents had wired me plane tickets, but I never got them because, by that time, there was no postal service to speak of in Israel since the great majority of men and many women had been mobilized.

Nations were coming against Israel. The crowning blow was May 22, 1967, when Egypt blocked the Gulf of Aqba. Rafi waited impatiently. Daily, men were being called up so that fewer and fewer men were in the *merkaz* on *Erev Shabbat*. Rafi, like all the young men in our group, was passionate in his patriotism. He was glad to finally be called up, and he left.

Life went on as normally as possible with the skeleton presence of men. I continued teaching in junior and senior high school and serving in the *moadone*, as usual. In both places the youth were getting more and more anxious about their fathers, brothers, cousins, and uncles leaving and being in danger.

Teaching English gave me an opportunity to teach them a song and encourage them at the same time.

"Let's sing a song to celebrate your fathers, brothers, and uncles in the army. Tell me the name of your brother in the army." I pointed to one after another so for the next weeks we daily sang a version of, "When Johnny Comes Marching Home Again," that I improvised.

"When Shlomo comes marching home again, Hurrah! Hurrah!

"When Shlomo comes marching home again Hurrah! Hurrah!

"We shout and dance and sing a song,

"We're sad today but it won't be long,

"And we'll all be glad when Shlomo comes marching home."

They loved it. We went through every mobilized father, brother, cousin, uncle, and the students never tired of it.

I assigned writing topics about the war and their feelings. I have kept the essays on two subjects all these years: "Do you believe Israel will win the war? Why or Why not?" and, "Do you believe in miracles?"

The content of the essays about the outcome of the war were strong and unanimous: "Of course, Israel will win the war. We are the strongest and the best military power in the world." As for miracles: "No! I do not believe in miracles. They are fairy tales for children."

With Rafi and most of the men gone, I spent my time after school helping the immigrants prepare for war. The Sephardic immigrants in Ashdod did not want to take any precautions. Their children were in danger, and the parents wanted to die along with them. They were paralyzed with fear and pain. These were not Sabras, used to Israel and used to fighting to protect their borders. These were not *Ashkanazi* Jews (European) who had been through the holocaust. These were North African and Middle Eastern Jews who had been chased from their countries by anti-Semitism. They were crying, wringing their hands, refusing to do the war preparation that we were all told to do.

We had been told to paint our light bulbs black and tape our windows to protect against shattering glass. Ashdod was a city on white sand, three minutes by air from Cairo. We were clearly in danger, and we all had to participate. So I helped with window and light bulb preparation and also with the sandbags and the ditches, which would serve as makeshift bomb shelters.

Rafi's brother had been called up, as well, so his wife and I spent long evenings and *Shabbat* with their anxious mother.

I had become such a fixture in Rafi's neighborhood that everyone there knew me. Tension was high. Rafi's mother leaned on me. She had two sons gone, so she relied on me and Eli's wife for comfort, because her husband had never ceased his unkind ways since marrying her when she was a child.

Footprints

God gave me the courage to stay.

I did not know then that the Christian walk requires great courage in the face of persecution. This was a test. I passed it. I don't believe I ever again, in life, had to make a decision that could cost me my life. I would later remember Esther, who fought her own fear, remembering the words of her uncle Mordecai: *"For if you remain silent at this time, relief and deliverance for the Jews will arise from another place, but you and your father's family will perish. And who knows but that you have come to the royal position for such a time as this?"* (Esther 4:14 NIV)

God is no respecter of persons, and His mercy endures forever.

He loved me no less when I was murdering His baby. He loved me no more when I was defending His Israel. He loves. God is love. We can do nothing to make Him love us more.

We can do nothing to make Him love us less.

And we have come to know and have believed the love which God has for us. God is love, and the one who abides in love abides in God, and God abides in him (1 John 4:16 NASB).

June 5, 1967— I walked out the door on the way to school and, as I started across the sand, I heard a siren (not the kind of sound I was used to in the USA, the slowly undulating whine, but rather a shrill sound), the kind of sound I heard in movies about Great Britain during World War II. *Well*, I thought, quickening my steps, *at least they are finally going to train us*. They had been promising to give us air raid practice.

Wait! I saw women rushing with baskets on their heads. With a jolt, I stopped walking and sand swirled around my feet. I started up again, increasing my pace, almost running through the heavy sand. As soon as I arrived at school, I joined the other staff and students entering the school, faces taut with concern. I climbed the steps to my classroom and settled the students.

The bell rang to signal the start of school. Then the intercom crackled to life.

"Israel is at war. The following nations have declared war on Israel."

By this time, I did not need a translator to understand the Hebrew. One after another, he named every Arab nation that surrounded us. Since then, history says Israel initiated the war. I am telling you what I heard on the intercom that morning.

"Here is the stand that the countries of the world are taking." The voice named the countries. It came to *L'Eretzot Abreet*, the United States. "Neutral."

Israel! It was so precious to me. What I thought of as an adventure when I left home had become Israel, the land of God's heart! Jerusalem! *My* Jerusalem. My heart swelled with reverence for *Ha Eretz* (the land).

My blood stopped flowing. My nation of birth: neutral. In the face of eleven Arab nations at war with Israel, the USA declared neutrality? A hard layer formed over my heart toward my birth country.

My mind went back to the long table at which we had all sat before beginning our adventure as *Sherut La'am* volunteers. Columbia University had created a form for us. That question suddenly appeared before me in bold black and white. Which do you consider yourself first? An American or a Jew? I had so boldly and automatically checked American.

Fingerpointer

Satan, the accuser, the mocker, laughed into my ear. That's your country. Your country doesn't stand up for Israel. What do you think about that? Hahahaha! And you are going back there.

I consider myself first a Jew, I thought, and saw myself unchecking one box and checking the other.

There, on the second floor, with war declared, my students stood stiffly, too agitated to sit; anxious, not for themselves, but for the whereabouts of their mothers and younger siblings.

"Proceed immediately to the bomb shelter. You will keep your students there until it is dark outside."

With Ashdod three minutes from Cairo by air and with the entire landscape being sand, every child would be a sure target. We directed our students downstairs to the bomb shelter, which was actually on the first floor above ground. The students took seats on the benches which ran the perimeter of the building.

"*Ha Morah* (teacher), when can I go find my sister?"

"*Ha* Morah, my mother is at work."

"*Ha* Morah . . ."

I felt so grateful—a sigh of relief—that I didn't have parents or a brother in Israel to worry about. I was alone in Israel. It seems strange to say I was glad to be alone, but I was. The anxiety among the youth was not for themselves but for the safety of their loved ones.

"Just think, Cheryl, if you die in Israel, you will die among strangers." I brushed that thought aside.

Songs began and peace settled. A singer named Naomi Zemer had recently produced a song called, "Yerushalyeem Shel Zahav" (Jerusalem of Gold), and now the lilting voices of Israeli teachers and children filled the bomb shelter. The song itself seemed to be a miracle to me. In May, Naomi had written it about Jerusalem, which was under Jordanian rule. Jews had been forced to leave two thousand years prior and were not allowed to visit their Holy City. So that beautiful song was sung in every bomb shelter that day about the longing in the heart of every Jew for Jerusalem.

We had no idea that by June 7, Jerusalem would once again be under Jewish control and Jews could enter their precious "City of Gold."

Footprints

If I forget you, Jerusalem, may my right hand forget its skill. May my tongue cling to the roof of my mouth if I do not remember you, if I do not consider Jerusalem my highest joy (Psalm 137:5–6 NIV).

Dark came, and we were able to accompany the children to places where other members of their families were also assembled, and we watched them hurry toward their homes. Suddenly, I wasn't so sure how happy I was to be alone. It was pitch dark as I walked across the sand back to the block where my apartment was. My mind kept circling the thought: *Die, yes. But be maimed?*

After stopping in my apartment to take off my shoes and put on my sandals, I went back out toward the building where the few of us who had not evacuated had decided to meet. But in the total blackness I was disoriented. I couldn't see a thing and didn't even know if I was headed in the right direction. My heart felt as if it were in my throat, and I felt numb and breathless with fear.

"What am I doing?"

When I decided to stay for the war, I was thinking long term to help tend the wounded. It was one thing to die for Israel. But what use would I be if my legs were blown off?

Fingerpointer

Yeah, you're really brave. All talk. "Jerusalem, I love you. Israel, to die for you is to die for God." But how would you like to live without arms or legs? How would your parents like to see you walk off the plane with bloody stubs? Hypocrite! Chicken!

This was the Accuser spitting out disdain.

Ah! I finally heard some familiar voices and entered a black room where the small group was gathered. The next day, we walked to the war office in the city and asked how we could help. We were politely refused. Israel did not want help from any of the Americans who were in the waiting room.

One man was indignant.

"I am an expert in removing tanks and aircraft from the desert. I have experience! They won't use me."

I found plenty to do, even without the government's approval. Bomb shelters were scattered throughout the city, and I went from shelter to shelter with a basket of crafts, coloring books, and crayons. Such bravery in those bomb shelters. In every one came the sweet sounds of "Yerushalyeem Shel Zahav" and other nationalistic songs about Eretz Israel. But not among the small dwellings of Ashdod immigrants. As soon as a mama got news that her son was killed, she would stand in the street wearing her traditional black garb, bloody scratches marking her cheeks where she had clawed them, her eyes hollow with despair, the grief of the ages in her wails.

Rafi's sister was lonesome for her husband and seldom put down their chubby adorable son. Little Gadi developed a cough that quickly became worse until he had trouble breathing. I told Sofie that we needed to take him to the doctor. We were in the midst of a tense mobilization, blackouts at night, nerves on edge. When we walked into the clinic, the doctor was curt and refused to examine the little one despite the child's obvious breathing distress.

"We are in the midst of a war! We need to shut down everything. I can't take time for this child!" For the first and last time that I was in my beloved Eretz Israel, I pulled the American card. By this time I was fluent in Hebrew; no one would have guessed my nationality by my accent or clothing.

"I'm an American, and if you don't examine this child, I will tell my nation that Israeli doctors don't care about the lives of children."

He hesitated less than a minute and took us into his office, examined Gadi, treated him, gave him medication, and we saw a quick recovery. *Baruch Ha Shem*! (Praise the Lord!)

In Ashdod, we had no word on what was happening in the war. My parents did, but they only heard lies from the Arab media. I found out later that when my mother saw Tel Aviv in flames on her nightly news, she threw herself on the ground and screamed. How could she know it was a lie? We found out after the war that no enemy plane entered Israel during that war.

On June 8th, I walked through *merkaz* to make a purchase for Rafi's younger sisters and mother. I heard the roar of a plane so close I could see the bottom of the aircraft right above my head. A couple of men, who had not been mobilized, were walking a few feet from me. They grabbed me, flinging me through the doorway of a shop. We had no idea that those planes were not enemy planes. They were all ours. Israel had wiped out the enemy's airplanes on the first day.

We were so proud when we heard the results. Golan Heights was taken. Thank God! No more bombing the children on the *kibbutz* at night.

Remember when I visited Shoshana and she told me how the children had to be taken to the bomb shelter every night because of the gunshots of the Syrians aimed at the children's houses? No more!

After the end of the war, stories came out. Whether they were true or not, I don't know, but they circulated. One was that Israel didn't have enough tanks so they made big cardboard cutouts of tanks and scared off the enemy attackers. Another was that Israeli soldiers banged on and broke pots to scare the enemy away. Yet another was that the Russians gave the Arabs very complicated planes, but the Arabs didn't know how to use them.

Chapter Twenty-Two
Let Us Go Up to Jerusalem

Finally, one *Shabbat,* Rafi walked in the door, exhausted, threw his packs down, hugged me and his family, flopped on his thin mattress, and fell into a deep sleep. He was not in the mail room as he had told me, but was, in fact, a tank commander in the Sinai Peninsula. In Israel, the tank commanders ride on top of the tank. My heart was so proud. He returned to the front for a while and then came home for good.

We heard the shouting that the war was over. Not only had Israel won, but also we had recovered Jerusalem. Everyone made plans to go *up* to Jerusalem, including Rafi's family. And everywhere they went, I went. Traffic was more than bumper-to-bumper. It seemed that the vehicles were stacked on top of each other as we made the ascent to Jerusalem.

What a sight! For the first time in two thousand years, Jerusalem was under Jewish control. Oh, to walk those streets! We were like ants in those walkways, squashed between bodies, animals, and cargo. There were Arabs selling drinks out of big metal urns that they hooked over one shoulder, pouring liquids into the two cups they held in the other; donkeys led by their owners; men with refrigerators on their backs. The Arab men were like beasts of burden. No trucks for them. No trailers. Backs. Their backs held the huge kitchen appliances or pieces of furniture strapped around their middles as they walked, bent over almost double to the ground. There were people everywhere as we walked through the gate into the Old City.

Late afternoon *Shabbat* was approaching so we parked in front of the home of Rafi's sister and brother who lived in the part of Jerusalem where Jews were allowed to live after the Jordan capture. They lived in a stone building with a cave-like quality to it. Like the rest of Rafii's family, they were Orthodox, so when *Erev Shabbat* came it was lights out.

The most frustrating thing was that it was "that time of the month," and I was in the bathroom in the pitch-black and couldn't take care of my business because I couldn't see a thing. Rafii broke *Shabbat* rule for me by giving me a flashlight. I'm not proud of that now, but at the time it made me feel special.

 Fingerpointer 

The thought echoed in my mind. *You made Rafi break the Sabbath. You are such a commandment breaker. There's nothing good about you.*

Satan is an instigator, a blamer, a mocker.

He sneered. "Oh yeah, oh great, you're in the dark and you can't even see in the bathroom. Then you made Rafi break the Sabbath for you. You worthless girl. You aren't a real Israeli, sniveling because you can't see in the bathroom."

Later, Jesus reminded me that He made the Sabbath for my benefit, not for its benefit. The Sabbath is a time of rest and enjoying the presence of God—not a time for keeping endless rules.

***Then he said to them, "The Sabbath was made for man, not man for the Sabbath. So the Son of Man is Lord even of the Sabbath"* (Mark 2:27–28 NIV).**

Rafi's sister served the typical family *Shabbat* dish called *cholent*, a stew that she started cooking twelve hours before *Shabbat*, then left on all night because no one was allowed to turn fire on or off on the Sabbath. The *Sephardic cholent* consisted of barley, beans, and a whole egg, which had turned brown by the time we ate.

After we returned from Jerusalem, Rafi asked me to marry him and gave me a ring. His mother and father were ecstatic, although his mother had told him months before to let me go.

"Shula is not strong enough to be a wife."

Nevertheless, she rejoiced and prepared to grab a live chicken and swing it over our heads. I don't know how, but I gracefully escaped the chicken swinging ceremony. I wouldn't have hurt his mother's feelings for anything. Some Orthodox Jews swing a chicken over the heads of the penitent and believe that the sins are passed onto the chicken. Then the chicken is slaughtered, which is observed as part of the chicken swinging ceremony.

Our engagement was bittersweet. I planned to go back to the States and change my major from psychology to English. Rafi would save money and, when he had enough, he would come to the US, where we would marry. Then, we would return to Israel to live where he would continue to work and I would get a job teaching English.

The day came to leave. I didn't want to go! I was leaving my nation and the father of my dead baby. Waiting to get on the plane, I sobbed and wailed like a woman who saw her child killed in front of her. Rafi was embarrassed. I ignored so many warning signs: he coerced me into sex, he wouldn't marry me, he hushed me when I wanted to love my baby by patting my abdomen, and now he was embarrassed by my grief.

Footprints

The abortion left such a chasm of pain in me, but God would use it to open the hearts of many women . . . many years later.

"I tell you, her sins—and they are many—have been forgiven, so she has shown me much love. But a person who is forgiven little shows only little love" (Luke 7:47 NLT).

"Shhh."

I couldn't stop crying. The plane took off, and I was on the way home to the USA. My parents had no idea what I had gone through. I got off the plane at O'Hare, and my mother walked right past me. She had said goodbye to a healthy, plump, smiling co-ed, and she didn't recognize this thin young woman with a haunted face. Suddenly she reeled around.

"Cheryl?"

I flew into her arms and fresh tears fell.

"Cheryl? Cheryl? I wouldn't even recognize you. You are scrawny. You are shriveled. You're like an old woman!"

We went down to baggage claim. I had given most of my belongings to Rafi's family and to my impoverished neighbors.

We pulled into the driveway, got out of the car, and walked into the house. There in the living room was a huge vase of flowers from Sinai Temple Sisterhood. They, who had begged me to come home before the war broke out, now considered me a hero. I wanted to sleep for days, but my mother insisted I go out with their friends the next day.

Chapter Twenty-Three

Exhausted, Stressed, Broken Down

"Mother, please, I can't possibly sit and make small talk. I'm exhausted. Please. Can we wait a few days?"

"No! We are going, and we are going tonight. We have reservations with three couples, and you are going, so get dressed."

We sat in Maxine and Heine's, a familiar restaurant, at a round table near the back of the restaurant. It was as if I could hear the women's voices through thick gauze.

"I like a lemon sauce on my shrimp."

"I have had a basil sauce but they were broiled."

"Chilled shrimp are lovely served with . . ."

What a stupid conversation! I thought, rage rising up from within me. *People are dying all over the world, and these women are talking about shrimp sauces! Bombs! Attacks! Children in fear!*

I felt myself moving—sliding off the chair, falling to the floor and collapsing, lying limp. I felt myself being half dragged into the bathroom where women made unintelligible, garbled noises around me. I felt damp cloths being placed on my head and being led back to my seat. One of the dinner guests was a physician and gave my mother some tranquilizers for me to take when I got home.

We left immediately, and when we walked into the kitchen, I took the pill my mother handed me and went right to bed.

But something was wrong. I suddenly awoke. My mouth was stretching open, way too far. I couldn't close it. I couldn't breathe. Then, without my effort, it slowly closed and then opened again wider and wider and wider.

I was in a panic and walked to my parents' room. I knocked on the door, stood by my mother, tapped her on the shoulder, and pointed to my mouth making some animal utterance trying to say, "I can't close my mouth."

 *Fingerpointer* 

It was as if the mocker was letting me know that I could open my mouth as much as I wanted, but I wouldn't be able to reveal the source of my pain.

I was an odd combination of terrified and numb.

"Joe! Get up! We're taking Cheryl to the hospital!"

We arrived at the hospital, and I was taken into a room in the ER and put up on an examination table. The nurse started asking me questions as if I were a small child, and I snapped at her, attempting to say, "Don't condescend to me," but what came out was a guttural mass of vocalization with no consonants or distinguishing the words because I couldn't close my mouth.

"We're admitting her as a hysteric."

I wanted to snap back at her, but knew I couldn't be understood, so I just closed my eyes. I was administered a drug that immediately stopped the spasms in my face, my mouth. Was it a reaction to the drug? Perhaps. But I think it was something deeper, something to do with an unspoken, horrific secret that I couldn't vocalize.

I was admitted into the hospital and, as was typical, my mother brought her book and knitting and planted herself beside me for as long as it would take for me to get well. She watched as I sat looking at the chicken on my plate.

Always the caregiver. My dear mother. She was faithful and loyal to my dad in the hospital, to my brother, to me. She was there from dawn to dark. Knitting and waiting.

"Aren't you hungry?"

I looked into her eyes. "I don't have the strength to eat it."

She bounded out of her chair and proceeded to cut the meat and feed me. She happened to be gone when Dr. Milne, my wonderful physician, came in.

"So Cheryl. What's going on?" I told him I had an abortion, and that I had to walk two miles across the sand afterward and bled and got very weak.

"You could have died, Cheryl!" he shouted. To my knowledge, he never told my parents. Once that ugly secret left my heart through my mouth, my strength returned and I was able to go home.

I had been 78 pounds when I left Michigan City for Indiana University after my summer diet. But after two years of starchy dormitory cafeteria foods, I had plumped up to a size 10. After the year in Israel, between the strenuous schedule on the *kibbutz*, the walking two miles a day on sand, and illness, I had shriveled to a child's size 6X.

Footprints

My body may have been the size of a child, but there was nothing of the child left in me.

The girl who had jumped off the tricycle and played the ukulele on the sun roof of the dorm was gone. Shriveled up and blown away like chaff from the wheat.

The painful lessons. It would be decades before I would comfort women according to 2 Corinthians 1:4. Jesus comforts us in our troubles. We can take that comfort and comfort others with it. But I didn't allow myself to be comforted.

It was decades before I allowed myself to think I deserved comfort for murdering my child. Once I was comforted, oh, the difference.

I left the hospital and, once again, became part of the Jewish community.

I seemed to be a heroine.

"You're so brave."

"Oh, thank you for what you did for Israel.

They had just been urging me, "Come home!" and now they were showering me with praise. I refused to accept it.

Had I accepted their gracious praise I could be welcomed back into the loving community, but the enemy whispered, *See! They're such fakes. They're so shallow. Get away!*

The enemy separates.

My father was a fiercely patriotic man. One of the joys of his day was to raise and lower the big flag on a tall pole in the common ground behind our house. Shortly after I got back from Israel, my pop poked his head into my room.

"Hey Cheryl, want to go with me to take down the flag?" It was something I always did with my pop.

"I'd rather burn the flag," I said flatly, the word "neutral" waving on its own pole in my mind. Quietly, he walked out of my room.

The enemy put words into my mouth that served as a knife to pierce my father's heart.

I spoke them without question, not once concerned about wounding the soul of the World War II veteran.

See how the enemy seeks to separate people from those who love them the most?

What a difference it would have made if I had stopped to tell Pop the story about being in the classroom and hearing, "The United States of America, neutral," when facing our *Eretz Israel* being demolished?

The enemy only separates, never works toward reconciliation.

Oh! For troubled teens to know this when they seek to run from loving families.

Later that week, we drove to friends of my family where many members of the Jewish community were gathered. We walked in and crossed through the many people who were standing and sitting as if waiting for a special occasion. My pop and I stood there in the small house filled with people I'd known since childhood. My face was flat and my arms were slack. Gone were all the lessons my mother had taught me about extending friendship: stepping forward, smiling, offering hugs. None. I felt myself standing as one dead. Why my father asked me to do this, I don't know. But he did.

"Cheryl, tell them what you said about the flag."

"I said I would rather burn it than fold it."

Gasps. Sobs. As one, the group stared at me. There were several veterans in the room. The Marshall Kottler *B'nai Brith* Lodge was even named after a fallen member of Sinai Temple. They were horrified as I stared at nothing.

"Cheryl, honey, I think you had better go."

 Fingerpointer 

More separation. More pain. More fingerpointing from the enemy.

If we could only learn to recognize it early. Does the thought leading to action promote reconciliation, healing, love, and the ability to move forward together?

That's the work of the Holy Spirit.

Or does the thought leading to action promote discord, anger, and make reconciliation harder?

That's a sure sign it is the voice of the enemy of your soul.

The hostess gently led me to the door. It didn't dawn on me until I was writing this: perhaps they were gathered to greet me? To welcome me home? What if I had behaved differently.

I could have told them I had been in the classroom when the war was declared and that the United States declared itself neutral. I could have said that when I left for Israel, I was American through and through—proud to be an American—American first and foremost, but that the year had made me love Israel, and when my country of origin turned its back on my country of heart, I couldn't fold the flag.

But I said nothing. The story was locked in my heart and couldn't find a way out of my mouth.

My mother and father were afraid that I wouldn't go back to college but would just wait for Rafi to come after he had saved the money and then I would leave with him. To their surprise, I agreed to return as a junior. I walked into the same dorm, but there was nothing of the frivolous, lighthearted girl who had bruises from a tricycle race. The bruises were darker, but they were hidden deep.

Chapter Twenty-Four
Culture Shock

I had noticed culture shock the minute we stepped off the plane for our layover in France. I had felt myself sliding over the floors. I had not stood on waxed or polished floors in a year. Then, in New York, as I stepped up to the customs window, I put my hand out.

"May I borrow your pen?"

Slam! "No one borrows my pen!"

And now, onto my college campus.

So much had changed. Before I left, there was no hippie culture. If someone were "hippy," she needed to take off a few pounds. There had been no expression, "Do your own thing." What thing? I was emotionless, quiet, and kept to myself.

There was one other Jewish girl on my floor named Susan, a music major. She mentioned wanting to help out their family finances by getting a job. That gave me the impetus to go to work, finally, helping my parents out who had paid all my bills in college since my freshman year. My parents were so gracious. The job I got paid pennies, but they acted as if I were doing them an enormous favor. My job: washing dishes in a boys' dorm. Disgusting.

To keep my uniform from dragging on the floor (remember me, 4'8"), I hitched the skirt up above my waist and tied the apron so that my skirt was lopsided and gave me a bulky-looking, clumsy middle. I passed some boys who spoke jeeringly, looking at me and another girl in the identical ugly attire, hers maybe a little less hideous because it wasn't bunched up and tied. Was I surprised to hear them speaking Hebrew!

"Chayot" (animals). I think they were more surprised to find out that I understood them.

"Ah! *Atem midabreem eevreet.*"

They turned scarlet as they understood my words. "Ah! You speak Hebrew!"

I took another job in the foreign students' department, doing some mailing; and another babysitting and doing housekeeping for a man whose wife was out of town. Then there was the catering job, hauling huge trays from the kitchen into the Indiana Foundation dining room for significant events. One notable event was the fortieth class reunion of Indiana University. Oh, they looked so bulging and old and wrinkled. And to think that, soon, I will celebrate my *50th* college class reunion!

I was passing by the table of a fat, probably drunk, man thoroughly enjoying himself when he saw me and yelled for the entire room to hear: "C'mere! C'mere!" he said, pulling me by my apron toward him. "Look! Look at her! She could have just stayed home and gotten a job in a dime store. And she chose to go to college. Just because she's short doesn't mean she can't learn." I could have fallen through the floor. It was bad enough to be 4'8", but to have it called to the attention of a roomful of men and women, even if they were drunk, was mortifying.

Fingerpointer

To humiliate anyone is the work of the enemy.

When we shame someone, use sarcasm or scorn, or share their flaws in public, we are the voice of the enemy who wants to thwart communication and goodwill.

Who could enjoy the company and share the heart with someone who scoffs and derides?

If we have the tendency to use humor for our own advantage—to get attention, seem clever—we may be getting what we think we need by crushing the soul of another.

The next week, we were catering a meal for an exclusive group of donors. Ten minutes before the beginning of the event, I stepped onto the floral carpet of the dining room and dropped my tray holding twenty-six plates of apple pie onto that beautiful floor.

Not long afterward, I went to the university clinic with severe stomach pains. A diagnosis of stomach spasms from carrying heavy trays clinched it. I was out of the catering business.

I was just waiting for the time when Rafi would come to the US and we would get married. Finally he did write that he had the amount of money that he needed. The week before Christmas, my parents and I left to go to the airport to collect him. There he came. Small, carrying a large pastel blue cardboard-looking suitcase. We took him home, me chattering in the backseat in Hebrew with Rafi whose English was limited to three phrases.

Two weeks into the visit, my mother met me in the hallway, tears in her eyes.

"Cheryl, he just isn't for you."

I knew it. I knew it was true. I told him later that night.

He held me and said, "Shula, lie on the floor. Let me get you pregnant. Then your father will have to take care of us." The memory of the abortion, him forcing me to kill my baby rather than marrying me, and now wanting to create a life to keep himself in the United States stabbed me. Bile rose in my mouth.

My poor sweet Pop bought Rafi a ticket back to Israel for $540.00. "Believe me; it's cheap," he said.

We took Rafi to the airport and said goodbye at the gate. I walked through O'Hare Airport, tears streaming down my face. They weren't the gulping, grieving tears like the day I left Israel. They were the lonely, heartbroken tears of *no more*. "I will never ever, *ever* love anyone as much or that fiercely again."

Footprints

To give a vow declared in anger is to lock oneself in a prison.

When you vow a vow to God, do not delay in paying it, for he has no pleasure in fools. Pay what you vow (Ecclesiastes 5:4 ESV).

When a woman says, "Never again. I'll never love again," or a student says, "Forget it! I studied and flunked the test. Never again. I quit!" We are locking ourselves into prisons of futures dictated from our past.

Jesus says: *"Do not swear by your head, for you cannot make one hair white or black. Let what you say be simply 'Yes' or 'No'"* (Matthew 5:37 RSV).

Every Saturday morning, my father met the guys at the local delicatessen. But, that Saturday he missed his breakfast date with his buddies for the first time. Maybe he was too embarrassed to try to explain the departure of my fiancé. My heartache seemed unbearable. I loved Rafi so much, but he wasn't right. He didn't fit into the culture. I identified with Genevieve in *Les Parapluies De Cherbourg*.

She was in love with an auto mechanic but, to her mother, a relationship with him was out of the question. Genevieve's mother had high expectations for status and financial stability for Genevieve. So Genevieve closed off her heart to the man she loved and instead married a wealthy businessman with the position and status that satisfied her mother. I could imagine the evenings that Genevieve would sit longing for the one man she would ever truly love while she was faithful to her mother's dreams for her. One afternoon, when Genevieve stopped at a petrol station, she saw him. Their eyes met, then locked. Love that would never be. She finished her transaction at the petrol station and drove away.

Two weeks later, I received a letter from Rafi.

"Just because I cannot dance and play the piano, I am not able to marry you. I will prove to you one day that I will be more than you think."

In preparation for filling in details of this book, I found Rafi in Israel and contacted him. He, indeed, did what he said he would. He worked long years to earn the money to go back to university, and he is now a successful professional in Israel.

Rafi was gone. Christmas break was over. I returned to Indiana University to finish my junior year. While other girls were going to parties and talking about boys, I stayed to myself. My eyes were haunted with memories, seeing scenes that took place eight thousand miles away.

In fact, I never did love anyone again in the same way I had loved Rafi. But life does have a way of going on, and the next semester I moved into an apartment with Susan, the Jewish girl who lived on my floor in the dorm.

Fingerpointer

See how that worked? I vowed never to love again, and I never did.

It wasn't until writing this book that I realized the power of that vow and the ability to break it.

Thank God, I am in love with my husband of forty-three years, though I didn't break that vow until I was into the forty-first year of marriage.

Footprints

There is hope! The hope is that we can break the vow as we break a curse by declaring the opposite.

For the person who was cheated against and had vowed never to trust again—that is a trap. If, for example, we vowed never to trust again, we can declare, "Lord, I vowed never to trust! I ask You to help me, Father, to open my heart to those whom You have sent to me. Let me develop the wisdom to understand and discern Your ways and walk in them."

Save yourself like a gazelle from the hand of the hunter, like a bird from the hand of the fowler (Proverbs 6:5 ESV).

My senior year, my brother, Jeff, came to live on campus, and that was the saving piece of life until I graduated. I saw Jeff totally differently. When I left for college, he had been a kid brother, but now he was a peer. I took such pleasure in showing him the ropes and having him over for dinner. Having my brother on campus was the best part of college life for me.

My parents had budgeted to have me finish college before Jeff started the following year, but my expensive year in Israel meant two in college my last semester. Fortunately, I had taken heavy credit loads so I graduated in three and a half rather than four years, so they only had two in college for one semester.

I moved back to my hometown, Michigan City, Indiana, to live with my parents. I interviewed for a position with Dr. A. K. Smith and was hired on the spot to teach French at Barker Junior High School, a position that would start in September.

In the meantime, I was able to do my student teaching with students taking French in grades seven through nine at another area school. I prepared the lessons for those young teenagers like the ones I had been studying as an upperclassman where classes were total immersion, and our readings had been classical novels in French.

The first exam I gave was on evaluating French poetry. The test I wrote was so long and so difficult that no student could pass it. I had worked so hard to get from "barely enough" to Dean's list every year that it was hard to come down to the level I was teaching.

Chapter Twenty-Five
Righteous Anger?

One morning, I walked into the teachers' lounge between classes where three male teachers were sprawled on the couch speaking hideous things about the black students, describing them in utterly disrespectful ways that had nothing to do with academics and everything to do with their race. I stood in the doorway and stared at them.

"How can you call yourselves teachers when you have utter contempt for students who are in your care? And to talk about their race like this. This is horrifying!"

Fingerpointer

We can cooperate with the accuser of the brethren when we judge. Was I acting as the fingerpointer by esteeming those gentlemen as lower than myself?

Do nothing out of selfish ambition or vain conceit. Rather, in humility value others above yourself **(Philippians 2:3–4 NIV).**

One of the men, a school counselor, rose to stare down at me. "You're calling us racists?"

"I'm saying that this is horrible. You are teachers, and you are in here saying despicable things about students in your care based on their race."

Every time the door opened and another teacher entered the teacher's lounge, the counselor repeated, "Cheryl says we're racists."

Black students. I don't know why I was drawn to them, but I knew that I wanted to help them succeed. I found them endearing and loved helping them do their best. One student even invited me to her house for a Labor Day family dinner party. I was touched to be invited. When I arrived at the apartment, it was packed, and I was the only Caucasian. I felt so honored to be included. I felt trusted by this wonderful group of people.

Two weeks later, I got a phone call from the state office that oversees education in Indiana. They told me that they wanted an appointment with me. So one day after school, they came into my classroom and identified themselves.

"There has been a complaint made about you. We hear that you are a flag-waver for the colored students. You should care about the education of all students."

"Flag-waver?" I said. "Can you explain? I care about all my students."

"We mean to say that it has been brought to our attention that you are a flag-waver for the colored students in the school. That should speak for itself."

In spite of the criticism, I changed nothing about my relationship with students. I loved them all. I helped them all. I continued to help African American students with a heart full of love and hope for them. No one ever brought it up again. Their little huffing and puffing didn't blow my house down.

Today, I live fifteen minutes from Ferguson, which seems to have drawn the eyes of the world on the relationship between African Americans and law enforcement officials. Satan used my love for the African American people to scoff at me and accuse me. *"You think you're all that. Yeah. The Great White Hope. What a joke you are."*

But I stand up and speak the truth—not to him—he doesn't deserve my response, but to myself: it is a good and wholesome thing to love a generation.

I'm grateful for God's love He has shed abroad in my heart. I'm grateful for the early years at Central School with a predominately African American population. Did I have to confront the men in the teachers' lounge? They didn't change. I stirred up a hornet's nest bringing in the State to chastise me. But I stood. I stood and I'm glad, and I would do it again.

September came, and it began. My teaching career. I was the junior high French teacher. To think that I had vowed never to be a teacher. I had labeled teaching as "Deadly. Boring. Dull-witted." Those of us in the disciplines at Indiana University disdained the education majors. My English major gave me a reputation in my own eyes of being an intellectual. Learning to do lesson plans and learning to teach elementary arithmetic and language arts were held in low esteem in my eyes, including everyone I knew who wasn't an education major. So, no *way*!

My father insisted that I be able to earn a living and forced me to get classes for teaching certification in English and French. Father knows best, and I have loved the privilege of being a classroom teacher. Every day of my life, I know I make a difference.

So there I was that first week. I was excited and stayed up half the night to prepare for my first class. I arrived ready. Lesson plans containing hours' more activity than I needed. Books. Drills. Nonstop work.

One young lady, as she left the class, stopped at the door. "Miss Samelson, don't be so rigid. Let your age work for you not against you." I was twenty-three years old acting as if I were a spinster schoolmarm. I took her advice.

"We are going to play a game today," I said as I entered the classroom the following day. I explained my idea for teaching verb conjugation using a relay-race method that I developed the night before. I explained it to the class.

"Miss Samelson, this is going to be *chaotic,*" said a ninth grade girl who was not of the mind that I should use my youth to my advantage.

"Oh, come on. It will be fun, and you'll learn your conjugations better than writing them twenty times."

The students got into teams of six. The first person went to the chalkboard and wrote the infinitive on the board. Going back to her seat, she handed her chalk to the second person who went to the board and wrote the first person singular. She returned and gave the chalk to the next student who wrote the second person singular, and so on. Soon, they were flying to the board and back. The first ran up to the board, wrote, flew back, handing the chalk to the second person, and finally the last would tear up to the board, write, and turn around, chalk in raised hand facing the class, face red from the excitement and exertion. The first team to finish won if all six phrases were correct: first, second, third person singular; first, second, and third person plural. Anyone finding an error following the first person could change one or all conjugations.

It was so *loud!* Screams of, "No! That's not right. It's –es. Change that. No! It's –ent." It was *so much fun!*

I could have disdained the young woman's advice because she was a teenager, because she was just a ninth grader, when I had a college degree. But, I was humble enough to receive her correction, and I am glad I did. I took it and used it the rest of my teaching days. I continued to act young long after I wasn't. I'm glad she wasn't afraid to speak up.

I loved including French history and culture. When we studied the Impressionists, each student chose an artist and gave an in-depth oral report about the artist's personal life so the artist became a human being as well as a famous name. Each showed several reproductions of the artist's work and posted them around the classroom. As part of the in-class quiz, the students identified and told about several paintings on the wall and the artists who did them. But the best part of the unit was when we went to Chicago to the Art Institute.

Parents drove several cars, and my driving companion and I drove another. The plan was to go to the art museum and then to L'Escargot where the students would order in French and enjoy authentic French cuisine. Parents parked the cars, and all the students walked into the Art Institute with the papers I gave them, which they were to complete by finding each Impressionist's work and filling in the required information. My students were ecstatic as they recognized the masterpiece of every artist on the sheet.

From there, we went to L'Escargot where they enjoyed snails. It was so much fun to see them in a formal dining atmosphere complete with fancy napkins, white tablecloths, and flickering candles. All of the students wanted to try snails. Some of the slimy critters hit the ceiling as they were coaxed out of their shells by eager hands. Oh, we had a great time.

By this time, I was dating an accountant—my driving companion—in my quest to find someone to marry who was going to be able to earn a living. No one could compare to Rafi, my handsome Israeli tank commander. One of the students gallantly made a toast.

"To Miss Samelson and Conrad (the boring boyfriend)." With that, the water glass hit the candle, which fell over, setting the artfully folded napkin into a blaze. The student was horrified, and she stammered her apologies to the waitress and offered to pay for the napkin. The waitress smiled as she put out the fire and patted the student on the shoulder. She looked around the room.

"One thing is for sure. This group is *not* from Chicago. You are much too polite." We had a lot to talk about at dinner. Not only did they exclaim over being able to recognize Renoir, Manet, Monet, Degas along with all the rest, but there had been a commotion.

"Please clear the lobby," a voice said over the intercom.

What was going on?

By this time, we had dispersed for some free time. I had allowed the students to walk freely though all the exhibits and meet back at the lobby at a specific time. A half hour before our time to meet, word had it that a nude young woman was doing cartwheels in one segment of the museum and that she had been contained in a closed off area.

"Oh, God! Don't let it be one of mine!" I was so glad to be reunited and find that all of my students were clad.

We piled into the cars and headed back to Michigan City. Those were the days before seatbelts, and we had four passengers in the front and four in the back. I was so busy talking to Conrad about the day and watching the crazy Dan Ryan Expressway, that I did not know until later that one of my students had stuck her bare fanny out the back window of my 1970 Chevy Caprice.

Chapter Twenty-Six
Teaching! A Joy!

The following year, I taught English as well as French. One of my favorite assignments was the children's book-writing unit. Having students in English class write books for children and then read to them is common now, but I had never heard of anyone doing it then.

I went to the library and brought in thirty children's books and assigned the students to find in each one:

a) title, author, publishing company, city, date;

b) if the illustrator was the same person as the author, what medium was used for illustrations;

c) for what age group the book was written;

d) if the book told a story or taught a skill;

e) poetry or prose; and

f) if a story, list the characters and their significance to the book.

The writing assignment: each book had to be twenty-five pages of text and illustrations. They worked painstakingly and the outcome was jaw-dropping.

Footprints

God had my gifting in place. To think I had not wanted to be a teacher.

God's plan for me had *teacher* written at the top, so He made sure that I developed a joy for it. God has plans for us that are good. And what a joy to walk into them!

"For I know the plans I have for you," declares the Lord, *"plans to prosper you and not to harm you, plans to give you a hope and a future"* (Jeremiah 29:11 niv).

I contacted all the early childhood centers and kindergartens in the city and arranged for seven visits. I had a diverse set of students because all the students in Michigan City went to one of two schools: one public and one parochial. I had those who were very bright, with every advantage, in the same class with students who were tough, angry, neglected, abused at home, and who brought their rage into the classroom. I had gifted and talented students in the same class as students who had IQs in the sixties or below. We were all together in the book-writing assignment, and no one let me down.

 Footprints 

"Write the vision and make it plain on tablets. That he may run who reads it" (Habakkuk 2:2 nkjv).

The instructions were plain. The students ran with it.

Dates were set for the school visits, and parents were scheduled as drivers. We piled into the cars, and in the event that parents didn't show up, the pre-seatbelt Ark, my 1970 Caprice, was crammed with kids piled on each other's laps. When we arrived in the school parking lot, they disembarked, patted down their rumpled clothing, and headed for the front door.

Depending on the school, we went into the library or gym; all my students were dressed for floor sitting. All my junior high school students sat in a circle on the floor, making their legs into laps. In came the little ones, eyes big, looking at all the teenagers who were proudly holding their books and smiling, some shyly, some broadly.

After being introduced, I began. "Hi, boys and girls. I have a special treat for you today. My very big boys and girls have written stories that they want to read, and they would love to read to you because they thought about you when they were writing their books. Would you like to hear a story that one of my big boys and girls wrote just for you?"

Oh, yes! Hands up! Eyes dancing!

One by one, I asked a child to go pick a guest reader. It was adorable to see a child shyly walk up to a huge teenager and plop down on a lap. Particularly endearing was seeing a big tough guy wearing a do-rag—which in those days weren't bought in stores but dragged out of mama's ragbag—sprawled with his big self on the floor and a big-eyed, sweetly smiling child plop down on his legs. The Michigan City newspaper picked it up, and the entire weekend special edition was devoted to the project. Oh, the pride in the hearts of the writers and their parents!

Another one of my favorite units was teaching students to write dialogue after watching soap operas and taking notes. First we watched segments of five soap operas and, as they watched, the students had to list all the characters and how they related to each other. We discussed the foolish plots, the ridiculous dialogue, and how real life is different. They, then, each wrote an idea for their own soap opera, which depicted their own lives. Each student read his or her topic and the summary. The class chose four script summaries to write, memorize, and perform in front of a parent audience. They got into teams to write out the scripts, with Stanley, the creator, serving as Director and the one to chose the cast.

The plots were exciting and true to the lives of teenagers living in tough times. Class periods were devoted to rehearsing the four stories that had been chosen to be videotaped in front of a live audience.

One afternoon, I got a message over the intercom: "Miss Samelson, you have a phone call that you need to take."

Oh, great, I thought. *Now what mess have I gotten myself into?*

I got a staff member to watch my class, and I walked to the office. Who could it be? I walked in, a puzzled look on my face, and the secretary mouthed, "A parent."

Oh no! Someone's mad because I'm showing soap operas.

"Hello?"

"Miss Samelson, this is me, . I told the secretary I was a dad so she would let me talk to you. I'm locked up. They let me make a phone call to you."

"Oh, my goodness, Stanley!" I could see his wheat-colored hair and his precious pink face. Stanley was a pill, and none of the teachers could handle him. He could easily have been the cause of teachers retiring early or leaving to work at Kmart, but for some reason, he loved me and perched on my desk every day. He was the writer-director of a play that was full of action about a group of juvenile delinquents.

"What happened?"

"I burned down a house trailer. But, Miss Samelson, I called about my play. Since I can't do it, could you have Derek be the director?"

My heart squeezed with a sweet pain that the play was so important to Stanley that he wanted to make sure it was in good hands.

I went back to class and confided in the students that Stanley was on the phone and he wouldn't be coming back to school that semester. "Derek, Stanley wants you to be the director." Derek almost cried. It was such a big deal to those kids. They got busy and practiced hard. When the day came for the play and videotaping, everyone was in character and everyone was proud. Grandmas came dressed in their best, hats and all. Dads took off work. It was an occasion. It was splendid!

I was a favorite with students, but with adults? I blasted my favorite music in the teachers' lounge while the older teachers were trying to work. No one confronted me directly, but there were a lot of raised eyebrows and meaningful glances at each other. It came time for the parent appreciation dinner and plans were in full swing. The shopping list included paper plates.

"We can't use paper plates!" I was horrified. "The parents deserve the best."

So the hunt was on for china plates, cups, saucers, platters, and bowls. It was a hit! Every teacher had prepared the family favorite, some handed down from generations. Everything was delicious and gorgeous.

At the end of the successful meal as the parents were leaving, one of the teachers said, "Okay, time to do the dishes," and tried to herd me in.

"Oh," I said, turning on my heel, "I don't do dishes."

I don't know why God does it. He blessed me, gifted me with so much, gave me a joy and zeal for life. Yet I was so rude and puffed up that I refused to do dishes. What was that? I got away with so much. But the time would come when He would tighten the reins.

The following year, I saw a brochure saying that foreign language teachers could take groups abroad. I went for it. I put a note in the bulletin that I would be taking a group of students to France the following summer. I received a phone call to come into the administration building and talk to the superintendent who had hired me.

Chapter Twenty-Seven

I'm Doing It Anyway

That afternoon, I drove from the junior high downtown to the administration building.

"Cheryl, you are a little young and inexperienced for this."

"Dr. Smith, I really respect you, but I'm going to take a group to Europe."

Footprints

It may have been out of order, but God had given me such a boldness to do what I believed I was called to do, regardless of my age. I had a way to go in the second part of the Scripture: *Let no one look down on you because you are young, but set an example for the believers in your speech, conduct, love, faithfulness, and purity* (1 Timothy 4:12 NET).

Chutzpa! (Guts, nerve) Five fifteen-year old girls wanted to go and had the money from their parents. But there was another girl who troubled me. She smoked, got into places with false IDs, and wore way too much makeup. Her mother had married a man only four years older than Arla.

"Hey, Arla," I said as the students were leaving for the next class, "would you like to go to France with us?"

Arla's usual breezy smile disappeared, and her face turned hard. "No way my parents would pay for me to go." She shrugged.

"Do you mind if I speak to your parents?"

I called and asked if I could come by and speak to them about something. They agreed, but when I walked into the house, it was a picture of "them" and "me." They were curled up together on a loveseat. I sat opposite. I told them about the great opportunity Arla had to go to Europe. Would they consider it? Could they pay half if I could raise the rest? They agreed to pay half.

I went back to school and told the teachers my plan. They scoffed and sputtered.

"Her! I wouldn't take that girl to a bowling alley. She's up to no good, and you are wasting your time and money."

Footprints

God has given me a heart for the least wanted, least loved.

"And the King will say, 'I tell you the truth, when you did it to one of the least of these my brothers and sisters, you were doing it to me!'" (Matthew 25:40 NLT).

I started planning by approaching the Foreign Language Club. They were willing to donate $200. We had popcorn sales, which brought in more money. Finally, I approached the principal about having an all-school dance and selling tickets with all the money going to her trip. He agreed, and it was an amazing success. I solicited and received certificates to restaurants, stores, and cinemas. I brought in a disc jockey, and the gym was decorated fabulously. Every thirty minutes there was a drawing. That Monday there was a note in my mailbox from the principal.

"Cheryl, congratulations on a job well done, bringing together the school community for a good cause," Mr. Dillon wrote.

Why did I go out on the limb for one girl when everyone said to forget it? Why did I work so hard for her? I saw something in Arla. I saw something worth saving. I saw that she was a young woman who could go either way . . . far! She could do great things or she could end up dead like my friend, the Bohemian. I took a chance.

I was determined to prove to Dr. A. K. Smith that I could do a fine job. I would bring home six healthy, intact, enriched young ladies. My first concern was not to lose any girls. None of these girls had traveled. To ensure that I could spot them, I insisted we all wear yellow dresses so we would be seen in the crowded airports. When we joined the rest of the group leaving for France, our group stuck out like a sunflower. We were bright yellow daisies in a field of bored, slouching jeans. (I know, I know! How embarrassing for them.)

The flight was easy, and we arrived in London for a week and then on to St. Malo, France, where we spent a month in an old monastery converted into a dormitory of sorts. The hard pillows of the huge beds were part of the mattresses. No plumping a pillow to get snuggled in for the night. The bathroom held huge tubs that could have given a monk a nice float.

From minute one I was on the job. No girl escaped my sight. I was a mother hen, an eagle eye, an elephant mom. I was twenty-four years old with a huge amount of energy, and Dr. A. K. Smith waiting back home to say, "I told you so." The other chaperones who were mostly from the East and West Coasts were "elderly," the average age being forty-five, and they were there for a good time. They let their kids go wild.

The older, seasoned chaperones had huge groups, some as many as thirty students in a group, which was lucrative because for every student over twenty they received $100. I had only six girls, so I had to pay for part of my trip. Those older ladies were there to kick up their heels. They were out of the house, away from responsibilities, and this was fun time for them. They did not seem to care for their charges. They never asked about their whereabouts, and I never saw them engaging in conversation with any of them.

I was a kid-magnet. One by one, the neglected teens from the free-at-last-forties groups found their way to me. My room was *packed*. I had girls sleeping everywhere. Some wanted to smoke in the dorm, which was totally forbidden.

"You'll get in trouble in there," I said. "If you're going to smoke, smoke in my room."

One by one, I heard the stories of their lives. Molly's father was a dentist. She had come with a toothache, and her dad gave her a douche bag to hook up to the door so that she could run water and antibiotics into her mouth.

Madeline, a pretty girl from Brooklyn, was not happy to be in France. "My parents sent me here just to get away from them. They dump me somewhere each summer."

Footprints

I would forever be looking for the one who was forgotten, ignored, unwanted, not enough.

"If a man has a hundred sheep and one of them wanders away, what will he do? Won't he leave the ninety-nine others on the hills and go out to search for the one that is lost?" (Matthew 18:12 NLT).

I am continually collecting women. Women with a Vision spans the globe. Women! It started with girls, with conversations about douche bags and summer dumping grounds.

The organization had made all the arrangements for our activities, one of which horrified me. There was a planned visit to the Moulin Rouge where the girls were to see a show and each receive a half bottle of champagne. I told the leaders that I felt it was totally inappropriate because in the United States my girls weren't old enough to drink. My concern was ignored, flicked away like an annoying gnat. We went.

The Moulin Rouge. The sets were amazing. Huge water tanks slowly rose from beneath the stage floor. Once it was at our eye level, enormous porpoises started to perform. Beautiful women swam around them and in some cases got onto their backs to ride them. Champagne was delivered, each girl receiving one-half bottle. My eyeballs seemed to be on rolling sticks, as they looked everywhere at one time to make sure my girls were not in harm's way. The students from the East and West Coasts seemed to be seasoned drinkers. My girls from Indiana were naïve.

I looked back at the stage. *Oh, I can't believe this.* The set had changed; the porpoise tanks were lowered down under the stage, and we were looking at a tropical scene. The women were dancing. They were all topless. *Topless!* Even their breasts were the same shape and size.

I was aghast. It was worse than I thought. I had no idea that the women were going to be topless. Oh! The stories these girls were going to take home along with their full-color programs. Dr. A. K. Smith. *Oy!* Disaster.

We left the Moulin Rouge very late and walked toward the subway. My heart felt as if it were alternately stopping and then throbbing in my throat. Two of my girls (not Arla) were totally drunk. They were stumbling and could barely walk. The seasoned, ignored-by-parents-under-the-care-of-footloose-forties seemed to be able to hold their liquor—not my girls. They were sick as dogs.

We arrived back at the monastery/dorm, got the girls into bed, and when we got up the next morning, I received news that made my blood boil. My girls who could not hold their liquor because they were not drinkers were being punished by the organization. They would not be allowed to go on a side trip to Italy.

I fought it. My girls were inebriated because they were innocent. They were naïve. The rest of the students had tossed down their champagne with gusto and no symptoms of drunkenness because they consumed alcohol (and apparently a lot of it) back on the coasts.

"Don't you see the idiocy of this? You're punishing my students for feeling the effects of alcohol because they are nondrinkers. The kids who drank at home didn't even feel the effect. This is crazy! You can't punish my girls for this!"

Fingerpointer

Just like the enemy: tempt the girls with liquor. They drink. Then they are inebriated and punished. He lures us in, we take the bait, and then he mocks us.

Wine is a mocker and beer a brawler; whoever is led astray by them is not wise **(Proverbs 20:1 NIV).**

The directors relented. The girls were allowed to go on the excursion. One of the students of the "unflappable forties" was claustrophobic, and either her leader didn't know it or she was unaware that travel under the Alps included being in a pitch-black tunnel for eight miles. For once, the chaperone had to pay attention. It would have been hard to ignore the nonstop screaming.

The Alps were beautiful, and it seemed strange to us all to be standing in snow and yet be warm. The tour of Versailles was special to my group because as part of the French history piece of my class, I had read to them a biography of Marie Antoinette from cover to cover so the girls were prepared for the tour of the grounds and home of the tragic queen.

The tour concluded, and we were ready for the study portion of the six-week program. Two weeks were touring and travel in France, Italy, and Switzerland, and four were for study in St. Malo.

We fell into a routine. We ate all our meals in the cafeteria. Morning was *café au lait* served in large, handle-less "crockery" into which equal parts of hot coffee and warm milk were poured simultaneously. Remember my admonishment, "No complaining about food?" Well, the first dinner in London was oxtail soup. The girls were good sports. In St. Malo, dinner always included large bowls of mussels, which were squishy and suspect because of the little tiny spiders hiding in the shells. I'm not a fan of mussels to this day.

I met two young women close to my age among the chaperones. One is an amazing artist, and I have a piece of her work on my wall that she gave us when

Neil and I got married. The name of the piece: *Masculin et Feminine*. We three chaperones were given the opportunity to study along with the kids but, oh, puhleeze. We were in France!

So, while our students were working away, we wandered around the stone paths, poked our noses into delightful tiny shops, sat in cafes, nibbled on delicate pastry, and sipped the world's strongest coffee.

St. Malo was built of picturesque stone. The people loved Americans, unlike the stereotypical French. They were quick to tell us why they loved us. It was because the United States liberated Brittany at the end of World War II. So we could have almost anything we wanted—except for a crepe recipe. As were most of the stores, our favorite *creperie* was built into the stone. We would come in from the sunny sidewalk and squint, as we walked into the dim light and sat at one of the four small, wooden tables.

At the back of the room was a grill. Sweating behind it was Mme. Crepe. Every possible crepe was available: breakfast, lunch, dessert. They were hot, fluffy, and filled to overflowing with fresh ingredients. *"Madame, nous pouvons, s'il vous plait, votre recette des crepes?"* we asked on our last day.

"Non!" There it was. No, in any language!

One evening, after we got the girls settled for the evening, my friend, the artist, and I decided to hitchhike into town. A man slowed his vehicle as he rolled up alongside us.

"Would you two like to go to a bar?"

 Fingerpointer 

Sin. Stupidity! Still doing risky things.

The enemy is never short on temptations to lure young people into sin, and stupid is the person who gives in. Oh, the shame of it.

***Remember your Creator in the days of your youth: Before the days of adversity come and the years approach when you will say, "I have no delight in them"* (Ecclesiastes 12:1 HCSB).**

We were all for it, so we rode off with him. When he came to the establishment he had in mind, he parked the car and signaled for us to follow him. We entered the dark room and found a table.

After a while, I noticed something strange. In darkened booths, men were with men and women were with women, kissing and touching intimately—and where was that guy who brought us? Nowhere to be found.

He dumped us in a gay bar! We must have looked frantic because a man asked us if we needed a ride somewhere. We were so desperate we said yes, and thankfully, he took us back to the monastery.

One day, the girls and I decided to go shopping in an art district. I loved looking around, as did four of the girls, but two wanted to go to the post office.

"Okay," I said, "we will wait here for you."

They didn't come back and, after an hour, we were frantic and decided to walk to the bus stop where we always met to go back to the monastery.

The two were nowhere in sight. We walked quickly to the post office and tried to trace the steps the girls could have taken to get to the art stores or the bus stop. Nothing. Nowhere.

My heart filled with dread, thinking of the lost girls, the parents of the lost girls, and Dr. A. K. Smith. I rushed the other girls back to the monastery. There, in the huge bathroom were the two who had slipped away, soaking in the tubs, washcloths on heads. My heart!

"Where were you?" we asked.

"We thought we knew the way back, but we didn't. We thought we would try a different route. We got so scared when we realized we were lost. We did have the address of the monastery though, so we found a shop owner and showed him the address, and he told us where to catch the bus. A lady from the shop stayed with us until we got on the bus."

Rita sank farther into the tub until she was submerged. Stacy took over. "When we got on the bus we gave the address to the bus driver, and he motioned for us to sit behind him and to the side so he could tell us where to get off the bus." Stacy sighed and sank; then Rita bobbed up. "We were nervous wrecks. I had some Valium so I took one and gave one to Stacy and here we are."

The remainder of the trip was a blur. But all my girls got back to the States in one piece.

And Arla? After Arla returned from Europe, suddenly all the teachers wanted to be her best friend. She went on to college and got a double masters' degree: French and International Business. That summer changed the course of her life. How could it be that I was so sure of what was right and good, setting the girls on track, keeping my eyes on them at Moulin Rouge, watching over them like a mother hen, and yet making such stupid decisions for myself? Did I think I was above the law? Or not valuable enough for safekeeping?

We landed, got our luggage, and I noticed my parents waiting for me at the gate. Where was the boring accountant who was supposed to meet me?

"Where is Conrad?

When I got home, I found the letter saying he left me. He was ending our relationship because he didn't love me. I stared at the letter, dumbfounded, because I hadn't seen it coming.

My mother tutted and clucked. "Oh, there are plenty of nice men. You'll find someone else in no time. You'll be fine."

I cried for about five minutes. When I got up, I went looking for my mother. She was in the laundry room sobbing into her hands, grieving for me. My poor mother—if she only knew what I was doing, how many of God's laws I had broken, how I beckoned pain to surround me because of my own rebellion. She didn't know, but I couldn't live that way without retribution, without consequences . . . and they were coming.

Chapter Twenty-Eight
The Wooing of the Lord

Summer was over, and it was time for the High Holy Days. Even though I had always attended the High Holy Days, this time, something affected me with a yearning so deep it seemed to hurt. It was Yom Kippur, the Day of Atonement.

During the ten days between Rosh Hashanah and Yom Kippur, we were to search our hearts and go to those whom we had wronged and ask for forgiveness. We were to go to God with prayers and fasting, confessing all the sins we could recollect in which we had sinned against Him and ask Him to show us those we could not see. I stood with everyone, and something happened. I don't even know if the words were spoken, but it is as if I heard the rabbi say, "*You are forgiven for the year, forgiven all of the sins of the year.*"

It was as if I had never sinned. I was forgiven!

"You are forgiven for all the sins this year. The slate is wiped clean."

Footprints

After I had the abortion, I saw myself as a sinner for the first time. Now, for the first time, I had a taste of longing for a Savior.

I, who had broken every one of the Ten Commandments, was forgiven.

I stood in front of the brownish-maroon chair in Sinai Temple next to my parents.

I felt the comfort of the tradition as the ark opened; the rabbi reached in and took hold of the precious Torah and turned to face us.

I heard nothing else.

"Forgiven."

I felt so clean. I felt bigger on the inside, as if movers had gone in and hauled away huge masses of unwanted and unneeded furnishings. I was clean. I was cleared out. I was made new.

The following Friday evening a colleague and I went to O'Hare airport to pick up John, who was on the East Coast training for the FBI. I knew him barely, had only spoken to him briefly when he had substitute taught where I was teaching, but he had called and asked if I could give him a ride home from O'Hare Airport. I didn't feel comfortable driving on the freeway, but my colleague was willing so she picked me up and we went.

"Just drop her off here," John told my colleague, indicating his driveway. "I'll take her home." But when my colleague left and John opened the garage door, he didn't open his car door but pushed me down on a mat and got on top of me. Tears started streaming down my face as I realized what he was doing to me.

"For ---- sake! What is it?" he snapped.

I was choked with tears. "I was forgiven," I whispered through my tears.

I realized at that point there was nothing I could do to keep myself pure. I was no longer forgiven. I was stained forever. I must have caused this. Why did I even go to the airport? Why did I pick him up? Why didn't I let my colleague take me home? Those thoughts didn't even cross my mind.

My mind was echoing one phrase only: I had been forgiven. The Lord had wooed me in the synagogue by whispering

"You are forgiven" in that service. But here I was lying on that dirty mat. I had been so clean, pure, pristine, and just that fast I was filthy again.

Footprints

I saw myself filthy, but Jesus! Jesus was looking at His bride, trampled and used, but His, and one day, He would take me by the hand.

For now we see in a mirror, dimly, but then face to face. Now I know in part, but then I shall know just as I also am known (1 Corinthians 13:12 NKJV).

I wasn't even seeing in a mirror dimly. I was seeing filth. I was not seeing a glimpse of a Savior. I was seeing my sin. But God never left me, and His footprints were getting just a tiny bit visible.

Even though the enemy set me up, it was a good thing to know there was nothing I could do to save myself.

I went through life numb. I was disillusioned with love, having said goodbye to my Israeli forever-love-of-my-life, dumped by the accountant, and stained by the FBI agent-in-training. And the Marine? He came by a month after I returned from Israel. My father saw him coming and spread himself across the doorframe as if to prevent him from entering.

"Cheryl, if you still will marry me, we can get married next month," he said.

It's a good thing I said no, because the next month his wedding photo was in the newspaper.

My boyfriends seemed to be one disaster after another. So, I stopped looking for another one. I couldn't even imagine being a wife and mother, anyway. I put all my energy into teaching and forgot about romance.

"Cheryl, this looks like fun—something you would enjoy," my mother said as she pointed to a notice in the Sinai Temple bulletin. The Follies was to be an extravaganza with a director and costumes flown in from New York. There were several performances and, after the costs, all proceeds would go to the Temple as a fundraiser. I went, auditioned, and was cast in several scenes singing and dancing with groups. Great fun. There was one partner dance. I was matched up with a guy named Neil. He had been divorced for a month and a half, was scraggly and dirty looking with shoulder length hair. He had just gotten out of the hospital with a kidney stone, and he smelled ripe.

Chapter Twenty-Nine
Whatever You Do, Don't!

"Whatever you do, *don't* go out with Neil. He is divorced and has children. You are just way too selfish to get involved with anyone who has children."

My mother had told me about the Skids, this "cute little couple," while I was in Israel. I never gave them another thought, and here I was, a partner with the very "Skid" my mother had told me about, who didn't look at all cute. And now she was telling me to stay away from him.

After rehearsal one night, Neil invited me to his bare, ugly apartment. After he offered me a seat on his uncomfortable couch, he put on a 33-rpm record of Russian marching music. We listened to the whole thing, and he took me home. Date one.

The next time he took me to his apartment for a home-cooked dinner: Betty Crocker's Beef Stroganoff out of a box. My mother had told me never to let any man know I could iron or cook because he would take advantage of me.

"How about putting a pot of water on to boil?"

I looked at him, for once obeying my mother's advice. "Sorry. I don't know how to boil water."

We ate, and he took me home.

As we got to know each other, I realized how important his Judaism was to him. He knew so much. I thought, *If I marry Neil, he will teach me about God.*

We were married by Rabbi Richter in Sinai Temple in Michigan City, Indiana. We stood beneath the *chuppa* and recited our vows. Neil broke the glass under his foot, and we left for the reception. My parents had given us a lovely wedding at their country club. Guests entered the reception room, greeted by a jazz ensemble and champagne, and then took their places to receive a beautifully served dinner.

After the toasts and dancing, Neil's cousin and brother drove us to Chicago where we would stay at the Hyatt Regency and fly out the next day for Bermuda, paid for by my savings from my teaching job at Barker Junior High School. His idea of a honeymoon had been to take me to the Ozarks.

"The Ozarks! No way!" The Ozarks! Not good enough for me. So I planned our honeymoon.

Fingerpointer

I wonder if that was a declaration, like a type of curse: *you are too selfish.*

I had never been selfish. But that declaration was disastrous in the way it acted itself out.

I didn't know enough to shrug it off and refuse to let it stick, as I did much later.

***Like a fluttering sparrow or a darting swallow, an undeserved curse will not land on its intended victim* (Proverbs 26:2 NLT).**

***"That's not good enough for you,"* said an inner voice to spoiled Cheryl.**

I was all too glad to agree with this voice and complain, not being satisfied with what Neil could afford. The enemy waved flags of *"You need better!"* in front of me, and I grabbed it.

Neil's favorite part of the day was dusk when we would stand on the veranda of the big, old, musty pink stone hotel and watch the manta rays slowly slice the water, making an arc around the expansive hotel front.

We had a regular seating at every meal, so we got to know a few people. One woman who befriended me was a spinster teacher of business from Connecticut. One day, she asked, "Cheryl, how do you get men to pay attention to you?"

I—the one who never says, "I don't know," because, unless it was math, I pretty much thought I knew everything—said, "You catch the eye of a man, smile briefly then look away. That's it."

 Fingerpointer 

My thinking that I knew everything was pride, and it stinks in the nostrils of the Lord. The fingerpointer lures us into pride and then slams condemnation in the next breath.

If anyone supposes that he knows anything, he has not yet known as he ought to know (1 Corinthians 8:2 NASB).

The next morning, the business teacher was not at breakfast. Mid-morning a man knocked on our door, "Do you know the lady who sits alone at table 10?"

"Yes! What's wrong? We noticed she wasn't at breakfast."

"She asked me to give you this note."

On the note was the name of a hospital and scrawled were the words, "Please come."

We immediately ordered a taxi. My heart was pounding. The taxi dropped us off in front of the hospital, and we hurried in and took the note with her name on it to the desk.

"Oh, yes. She's waiting for you. Go up to the third floor, and a nurse will meet you up there." A nurse greeted us and asked us to follow her. She stopped by a door and motioned for us to enter.

I would never have recognized her. Mildred was in a hospital bed, bandaged so that I could only see one eye. Her mouth was a mass of bruised flesh.

"It worked, Cheryl," she managed to say, attempting to lift herself up on her elbows to better see me. I hurried to the side of her bed, my hand over my mouth.

She told me the horror story.

"Last night I saw two Bermudian men, and I used your technique. They asked me to go out on a boat with them. I did. But when we were in the middle of the water, one of the men beat me and shoved me off the boat and left me. I grabbed hold of a piece of wood, and I don't remember anything else."

We found out from the nurse that someone had seen the light of the boat. The men were arrested, and she was rushed by ambulance to the hospital. The first thing she said when she regained consciousness was, "Tell Cheryl I did it."

I was undone. My own boastfulness had caused this disaster.

"Oh, my God! This is my entire fault. I taught you to flirt."

Her one unbandaged eye twinkled, and she said, "Cheryl, I have had an adventure."

Chapter Thirty
Loneliness

Sorrow and loneliness began on my honeymoon. When Neil stayed late to listen to the pretty singer in the lounge, I thought he was choosing her over me. When he spent time getting to know two hairdressers from Delaware, I thought he was ignoring me. I started and finished all 677 pages of *The Peaceable Kingdom* on my honeymoon. We arrived home August 18. My birthday was September 29. I lay on my bed and cried two hours. I felt rejected, alone, and so, so unhappy.

Footprints

Loneliness can be a sign that we are not as united as God wants us to be. Loneliness causes us to long for . . . for what? The object of our longing can end in disasters or delight.

Then the LORD God said, "It is not good for the man to be alone. I will make a helper who is just right for him" (Genesis 2:18 NLT).

Maybe I had been selfish and bent on having my way, being the center of attention.

It was several years before I realized that my loneliness was a call from God to come higher.

"Come up here, and I will show you what must happen after this" (Revelation 4:1 NLT).

This was spoken to John, the Revelator, but to all of us He says, "Quit looking at that small picture! Raise your eyes! Come up higher so I can show you what must take place."

It is as if He wanted to say to me, if only I would listen, "Something must take place in your thinking, your behavior, before you can reach the joy that I have for you."

Neither one of us was able to communicate in a healthy manner. One day, out of frustration, Neil picked up a large rubber tree plant and hurled it over his head. Clumps of black, damp soil flew all over my month-old white furniture in our beautiful new apartment with round walls. Another day, again frustrated, he slammed his fist into the wall.

I called my mother after the rubber tree episode, and she said, "It was just probably your big mouth."

I knew I was mouthy. I didn't control my mouth much at all and had gotten away with saying outrageous things. So I tucked that away as truth.

When the fist went into the wall, I hung a mirror over it. For the next many years I kept covering the signs of his frustration.

My mother probably was right. I was selfish, but I didn't recognize it until years later. I had lived my life thumbing my nose at authority and doing what I wanted, regardless of the feelings of others. I had always gotten away with it. Until now.

I immediately wanted a baby. My idea of marriage was having a little girl. Every month, when the proof showed that I wasn't pregnant, I cried. It really didn't take that long, considering what some couples go through, because nineteen months after we got married I found out I was pregnant.

I walked into the apartment excited about my news, holding the piece of paper. Maybe I should have waited until Neil was off the phone with his friend to tell him. I held up the paper and waved it, smiling, mouthing, "I am pregnant." He didn't register any emotion or give me any indication that he cared what I had to tell him. I put my hand on my tummy. "I will love you enough for both of us," I whispered, turning around to leave the room.

The enemy had sealed me into settling for an abusive relationship, thinking I deserved it because someone I trusted told me so. She meant only good for me. My selfishness and Neil's frustration worked toward torment for both of us.

Fingerpointer

That "I will love you enough for both of us" was a declaration that only I could properly love our children. That was a vow that wasn't broken for years until I realized Neil adored his children as much as I did. The enemy prompted me to think Neil wouldn't love our children, and I swallowed it.

It was March, so I had two months before I had to sign a teaching contract for the following year. I declined. I loved having my mother at home while I was growing up, and I wanted to be there for my children. I knew myself well enough to know that if I were teaching I would give it my all, and I wasn't willing to let anyone else or a day care raise my child. I determined not to teach while I had children under school age.

But, in the meantime, Neil and I had become fast friends with Barbara and her husband who lived across the hall from us in our apartment building. Barbara and I were both teachers, young wives, and childless, so we had much in common and enjoyed each other's company. The loneliness of the early days of marriage had lessened with a new friend.

But then, they bought a house. When she told me where, I was shocked.

"Barbara! How can you possibly purchase a house in Long Beach, knowing they're restricted against Jews?" I resented what I considered a personal affront.

Fingerpointer

Anger and offense. Two things that can destroy relationships for years.

Good sense makes a man slow to anger, and it is his glory to overlook an offense **(Proverbs 19:11 RSV).**

They did not intend to offend me in purchasing a home in an area that did not allow Jews, and it was not my business. To take on anger that doesn't have a constructive end is destructive. Offense lodges like a brick in the gut and can ruin friendships for a lifetime.

So the enemy saw his opportunity to destroy a relationship.

After they moved, I started to put pressure on Neil to buy a house, too. Even though our apartment was fine, every Jewish woman in Michigan City had a house, and I wanted what they had. Still headstrong. Still wanted it my way. Still not satisfied.

Footprints

Where jealousy and selfish ambition exist, there will be disorder and every vile practice (James 3:16 ESV).

Can you hear the enemy whispering to selfish, greedy, dissatisfied Cheryl? *"Now she has a house and you don't."*

We found a house in Edgewood, closing on it on Monday. The following day, Tuesday, was the day I held out my "I'm pregnant" note to Neil. The next day, Wednesday, Neil lost his job. So I was stuck with *my way*: a house I hated and a husband who was moving to a position for which he was immediately hired after losing the job. We would have to sell our house and move to Columbus, Ohio.

My poor mother. I can still see her. She had broken her arm while playing tennis. Nevertheless; she had knitted a blanket for her little grandchild who would soon be moving to Columbus.

Her eyes were red from weeping. I didn't know what I was heading for, or I would have been crying, too. Instead I was numb. I was left pregnant and alone because Neil's job started immediately, and I lived alone in a house that I hated because it wasn't even ours. Boxes everywhere, the first two months not even paid for, and we had to sell it, taking a loss.

"Cheryl, move back into our home. You don't need to sit in that house alone," my mother said when she dropped in and saw me staring blankly.

My dear friend was a godsend. Joanne lived at home with her parents and worked in Chicago, so she packed up and moved in with me until I finally left for Columbus. Having her with me made life somewhat bearable. Somewhat.

I never understood depression before it claimed me.

"Pick yourself up," I would say when others said they were depressed or couldn't get out of bed. "Just do something." But depression, like a heavy, gray blanket, settled firmly around me, and I had no strength to raise it.

Footprints

Sometimes what seems like an attack of the enemy is a wooing of the Lord to come closer, come higher. When we are oppressed or depressed, we can call upon the Lord.

The LORD himself goes before you and will be with you; he will never leave you nor forsake you. Do not be afraid; do not be discouraged (Deuteronomy 31:8 NIV).

But You, O LORD, are a shield about me, my glory, and the lifter my head (Psalm 3:3 ESV).

I wasn't thinking like that. I didn't feel the nudge of the Lord.

The house finally sold, and the ladies of Sinai Temple sisterhood gave me a baby shower as I planned to leave town with my mother's only grandchild in my womb. My mother looked so pathetic sitting there with her broken wrist, watching me hold up that beautiful blanket knitted with strands of her love. I was smiling, the darling of everyone in Michigan City. The girl who had gone to Israel and stayed during a war. The teacher whose projects were celebrated in the newspaper. A finalist in Young Business and Professional Women of Indiana. But my smile would be knocked off my face for decades.

Fingerpointer

"Yeah, you're such a darling of Michigan City. Let's see how you look with that face smeared on the pavement."

Who said I was the darling?

What chutzpa! God's Word warns against that grandiose thinking. If I had measured myself by faith rather than a couple of experiences, I wouldn't have been so high and mighty.

***Because of the privilege and authority God has given me, I give each of you this warning: Don't think you are better than you really are. Be honest in your evaluation of yourselves, measuring yourselves by the faith God has given us* (Romans 12:3 NLT).**

Neil's employer paid for packers and movers, and the day came to say goodbye to my parents. We drove off in the Chevy Caprice I had purchased the year before and in which I had hauled dozens of students to field trips. I drove that car for fourteen additional years.

Neil moved right into a working community. He left in the morning, went to a job he loved, came back, and after supper he headed for the tennis courts with the buddies he quickly made. I made no friends. All day, I sat in the town house, lonely.

One day, I saw a woman heading toward the dumpster. I ran out to greet her.

"Will you come visit me? I am so lonesome."

Footprints

My soul melteth for heaviness: strengthen thou me according unto thy word (Psalm 119:28 KJV).

My soul was melting for sadness, but I couldn't be strengthened according to God's Word because I wasn't opening a Bible. I wasn't thinking about God at all.

The woman dumped her trash, glanced at me as if I were an oddity, walked into her apartment, and closed the door.

My parents were due to visit us before the baby came. They planned to arrive December 22 and stay through Christmas; the baby was due January 12, 1975, Super Bowl Sunday. Why do I remember that? I had an aversion to sports and was secretly glad that I would take a bunch of men away from "the" game in order to be with me as I delivered our baby. What an attitude!

However, on December 22, at nine in the morning, my water broke.

Chapter Thirty-One

She Won't Recognize a Smile or Laughter

"Hi, Mother. I know you're planning to come today, but my water broke."

"Your water broke!" my mother's voice was shrill. "Where are you?"

"I'm here, in the kitchen, talking to you with a towel between my legs."

"Get to the hospital! Where is Neil?"

"He's taking a shower."

"He's taking a shower? Now? Get to the hospital!"

She was frantic for me. Her labor and delivery had been horrible, and she expected the same for me.

Neil drove me to St. Ann's hospital, and Amy was born at 11:30, only two and a half hours after we drove up to the door. What a little *pitzel*! I didn't know much Yiddish, but did know that *pitzel* means tiny little child. Her skiing down the birth canal left a red mark from the top of her forehead to the bottom of her chin. She was three weeks early, and her little top lip hadn't had time to come in. By the time my parents and Jeff got there, Amy Allison was all snuggled into her Isolette next to my hospital bed. The red mark faded in no time, and in a few weeks her little lips were perfectly plump.

On Christmas morning, my nurse brought Amy to me loaded into a red stocking. Much was made of the little tiny baby who was swimming in the white outfit my parents had purchased, then swallowed up in the big, white bunting lovingly made by Helen, a dear, older friend.

My mother, father, Neil, and I drove home to the apartment. I was so glad to have my family there that, rather than rest, I ran up and down the stairs of the townhouse at least twenty times the first day.

The next, I insisted on making my dad's breakfast. The movement slowed my recovery and caused considerable bleeding, but I was so grateful to have my family there that I didn't care.

Then, the day came for them to leave. It had been nine days.

"You can't leave. How can you leave? I can't take care of a baby. I can't even take care of myself."

I managed after they left, but I don't know how, so great was my growing depression.

When Amy was six months old, Neil's sons came for the summer. I so wanted to be the perfect stepmother. I went shopping and bought a carload of toys. Neil walked in and started shouting about the clutter. I felt stung. I was trying the best I knew how. I took care of Amy and the boys during the day, cooking meals, providing fun things to do in the apartment, and taking them to the pool every nice day.

Neil came home, ate, and headed out to the tennis courts, leaving me to bathe the children and put them to bed. It wasn't that I was resentful. I was just losing more and more of myself. I felt nothing. I started to feel that I must deserve this. From my mother's, "It's your big mouth," to the shame of being treated badly in my marriage, I eventually had no "rising out of the ashes" power.

Footprints

To all who mourn in Israel, he will give a crown of beauty for ashes, a joyous blessing instead of mourning, festive praise instead of despair. In their righteousness, they will be like great oaks that the LORD has planted for his own glory" (Isaiah 61:3 NLT).

The power was available, but I didn't know how to access it. I felt more and more devalued, wounded, abandoned, and I didn't know how to talk to God. I still was not thinking of Him at all.

One day, when my mother was there on a visit, she said, "Cheryl, Amy isn't going to know what a smile looks like or what laughter sounds like."

The phone rang, and I made no move to answer it.

"Cheryl, why don't you ever answer the phone?" I felt her concerned eyes on me but didn't turn my face toward her.

I had become more and more depressed from loneliness and rejection that I had stopped answering the phone, knowing it was no one who cared about me.

A couple of months later, my parents came again to stay for a few days. One afternoon a colorful note caught my mother's her eye as it came through the mail slot in the door. She picked it up, and when she read it to me her voice was animated.

"New mothers talk about it over coffee, Tuesdays at 10:00. Call Leenie." My mother touched my face so I would look at her. "Cheryl! Go to this."

I tossed the note aside, wanting to go nowhere. But, thank God, I went. It saved Amy's life and mine. That little group became my Columbus family, and it pulled me out of depression. Amy and I had friends.

That little group of women on Tuesday mornings was a model, in part, for what would become Women with a Vision. In fact, I can see that all the pieces of my life—foolish and wise, sinful and righteous, intentional and accidental—were used by the Father whose eyes never left me, ever. Because of that horrific year, I can understand about depression in women. I know that we can't just "snap out of it." But I also know that a network of loving women can pull us up and out, because it happened to me.

Footprints

Hope!

Hope deferred maketh the heart sick, but when the desire cometh, it is a tree of life (Proverbs 13:12 KJV).

I had a way to go before I realized that my hope is in the Lord, but this was a reprieve from the horrible depression.

Hope! How important it is to give people hope!

Chapter Thirty-Two

Turning the Corner of Hope

The Tuesday morning group was something to look forward to every week. We took turns getting out our dishes—some women used their best china teacups and saucers—and making a nice morning snack for the women, often from old family recipes. We were eleven women and babies in small townhomes happily talking about what matters to new moms.

There were challenges: Amy was tiny, and I had to take care lest she get flattened under mounds of babies. Mothers had different ideas about sharing. But, we were a group. We were alive, and we were happy. We got the men involved through an International Gourmet Club, which met monthly in each other's apartments. The men loved showing off their culinary prowess by creating complicated dishes of the chosen nation.

Neil started to cook, a love which deepened later and turned into a midlife career change!

God didn't leave Neil out. I was hurting and desolate, and God was merciful to me to lift the depression through the Tuesday group. He included Neil in the refreshing.

There is no way one of us could hurt and it not touch the other, because the husband and wife are one. When one hurts, they both hurt.

I knew nothing of that then and had no compassion on my husband, whose behavior made me feel horrible. But God's mercy surrounded us both.

Have mercy upon us, O Lord, have mercy upon us: for we are exceedingly filled with contempt (Psalm 123:3 KJV).

I knew nothing about God's plan for marriage, most of which is taught in the New Testament, but I know now that contempt from a woman is death to man's spirit.

Neil's continual anger toward me triggered my continual contempt for him. God gave us respite from time to time to keep our heads above water until we had sense to know what to do according to His Word.

When Amy was eighteen months old, I started thinking about a toddler enrichment program. I was taking her to baby swim, but I wanted more. However, nothing I saw impressed me, so I decided to start my own. I didn't realize what an ambitious project it was, but I wanted the best for my little girl.

First, I went to Ohio State University and made appointments with professors so that I could learn about reading readiness. Then I researched zoning. I studied curriculum. I advertised, using posters to display in children's shops and pediatrician's offices. That didn't come at once. I learned something valuable during that process. *Most people quit. Everything!* So, if I just kept plugging away, I would get "it" done, whatever "it" was. I determined to do one thing per day toward the goal of creating that preschool, and I did. It was a wonderful lesson in perseverance.

Footprints

The Lord was teaching me so many lessons I would need later.

Perseverance was one of my biggest strengths as I faced the battles ahead and pursued the call of God . . . later.

[Be]strengthened with all power according to His glorious might, for the attaining of all steadfastness and patience; joyously giving thanks to the Father, who has qualified us to share in the inheritance of the saints in Light (Colossians 1:11–12 NASB).

Sandbox Scholars was born! So now, I had a little preschool, friends on Tuesdays, and a gourmet club. Finally, I was fulfilled in many ways. Sure, I could have gone to work. I loved teaching, but I wouldn't be in the classroom full time until I had no children under school age because I knew I couldn't give the classroom what it needed if I were giving a child what she needed. With a little preschool I could do both. I was finally alive again.

Then Neil came home and told me he'd lost his job, but that he had been asked to come on board with a company in St. Louis. We were moving again. I felt the bottom fall out of my world—another first year in a new city. Neil moved to St. Louis. Once again the company sent packers and movers.

I told Sandbox Scholars' Moms that I was leaving and gave them instructions as to how to continue to meet on their own to enrich their toddlers' learning. I wrote a book with Amy about Daddy being gone and getting ready to move. White Dog, a stuffed animal given to her by my friend Joanne, looked remarkably like a tiny version of our one hundred pound Great Pyrenees, Avalanche. Amy loved White Dog and carried him everywhere, twiddling his ear and sucking her thumb. He was her security dog. He would not get packed.

I said goodbye to all my friends and made arrangements for my parents to keep Amy while I joined Neil in St. Louis for one week to find a house. I was determined to find a house in one week. I had made a list of things I required: sidewalks, so Amy could ride her big wheel (with me helping of course); a fenced backyard; a screened-in porch; a finished basement, so I could have another preschool; a window in the kitchen, so I could watch Amy from inside when I was doing dishes; a two car garage; and no trucks or vans parked in driveways or on the street. Armed with my list, I took off in the mornings and afternoons.

Within a week we found a house I loved. There were three contracts on it, but all fell through and it was ours. We have lived in that same house all these years, and it has served us well. I had no idea I would grow to love St. Louis. All

I knew was that, once again, I was wrenched away from people who had become like family. I lay in Neil's arms, weeping, that last Friday night in the motel. Our Erica Lynne was conceived that night. I had longed for another little girl to keep Amy company.

One thing I had learned from my mother and Sinai Temple Sisterhood is that if you want to meet people, you have to get involved and work together on common causes. Was it my personality? I don't know, but nothing clicked no matter how hard I tried.

One particular week, Neil and I wanted to go out to dinner with another couple. So I called all the couples I knew on the ORT group's list, but they all declined. The last woman I called said at the end of the conversation, "Can't you two just go out by yourselves? Why do you have to call all of us?"

I was so embarrassed.

Chapter Thirty-Three
A Child Made All the Difference

I needn't have feared loneliness. Those good friends of ours from Michigan City, who had lived across the hall from us, had moved to St. Louis a few years before, and they paved the way.

I quickly started another Sandbox Scholars. Having Amy in my life made all the difference in the second move. When I moved the first time, Neil was working and involved in his new job which he loved, while I was home with no friends, no job, and no baby. In St. Louis, I had my daughter, Amy. Her little two-year-old mind was always going. She was as smart as a whip and kept things interesting.

"I haven't found a better friend to hang out with than Amy," I wrote in a letter to a friend in Ohio. She was a delightful child and made life lively. Amy was my best buddy. She and I went everywhere together and, in addition to being great company, she opened the doors for lots of communication. She loved strangers.

Once, at the mall, I didn't realize that her little toes had popped out of her sandal. While I stopped her stroller so I could look at something, Amy got the attention of a nearby shopper, pointed to her foot, and engaged the woman in fixing her sandal. So really, the move to St. Louis wasn't as awful as I feared the night that I wept in Neil's arms.

I was invited to a card game up the street and, although I was not a card enthusiast, I went in order to meet some new people. Not thirty minutes after we sat down, one of the guests said, "I hate Jews," and went into a tirade on her experience with Jewish teens at her teaching job. I told her I was Jewish, but instead of being embarrassed she tossed her head with an, "And your point is . . . ?" look.

Now, I had been offended by the Jewish women in ORT in Columbus who didn't accept my overtures of friendship, but for someone else to talk about Jews hit me in the gut. With Jews, it's one thing for a Jew to tell a Jewish joke. It's another for a Gentile to do that. It's like family. I may think my sister is a pain in the neck, but don't you dare talk about her. So, that was an unpleasant moment.

Another, was shortly after we moved in. I was walking Amy in her buggy, making ruts through the mounds of snow that had fallen. A woman called out her door, "You must really be desperate to meet people."

Fingerpointer

From there Elisha went up to Bethel. As he was walking along the road, some boys came out of the town and jeered at him. *"Get out of here, baldy!" they said. "Get out of here, baldy!"* (2 Kings 2:23 NIV).

Ridicule is so painful, whether it is to a prophet like Elisha or a new mom like me.

So, Amy and I were the duo, inseparable. But, in my seventh month of pregnancy, when Amy was about two and a half years old, I went into premature labor with Erica. I went into the hospital where they stopped contractions and sent me home with instructions for bed rest, a prescription of paregoric three times a day, and a shot of alcohol three times a day—as in hard liquor. I was concerned about fetal alcohol syndrome so, on my next appointment, I took an article I found and asked my doctor about the risks of women who consume alcohol during their pregnancy.

"Which would you prefer? A premature baby? Their complications are far worse," the doctor snapped.

I thought back to when Amy was born, a little *pitzel* with a bright red streak from forehead to chin from her speedy descent down the birth canal being her only abnormality. That disappeared and the skinny lip plumped out, but what kinds of problems could this baby have if born two months early?

My mother came to spend two months with us, since I was ordered not to pick up Amy. My mother was a trooper. She left golf season at Pottawatomie Country Club. She didn't complain about it, but her teammates did, and I heard about it.

"How inconsiderate. It is golf season," whined a particularly self-centered friend of hers. So, my mother moved in and sat with me outside on the front lawn and drank with me: Bloody Marys, Scotch and soda, Vodka and tonic—three times a day, interspersed with my paregoric throughout the day.

Footprints

He who dwells in the shelter of the Most High will abide in the shadow of the Almighty. I will say to the Lord, "My refuge and my fortress, my God, in whom I trust."

For he will deliver you from the snare of the fowler and from the deadly pestilence (Psalm 91:1–3 ESV).

Now, I knew no scriptures except the Twenty-third Psalm, Psalm 121, and the expanded version of the Ten Commandments, but I could see God's hand throughout my life, looking back. Alcohol can be deadly to unborn babies and cause birth defects and behavior problems.

Erica had no symptoms of fetal alcohol syndrome, thank God.

It was the middle of summer in St. Louis, and when our air-conditioning broke, it was never fixed. Neil's job didn't last, and his work afterward wasn't steady, but I stuck to my vow not to teach with small children at home. The temperatures in the house were about the same as outside: 104, 105, and my body temperature felt double that. My mother was such a sport. She could have been in their lovely air-conditioned home, going to the country club, enjoying friends, but she stayed with me in our hot, tense home.

Footprints

A joyful heart is good medicine, but a broken spirit dries up the bones (Proverbs 17:22 HCSB).

Laughter later became a healing balm to me, but the brokenness of my spirit was drying me up.

I had attempted, and failed, to breastfeed Amy. She was nursed, but was continually fussy, crying and sucking, crying and sucking, so when she was five days old, I took her to the doctor. The doctor took her from me, gave her a four-ounce bottle of formula, and she sucked it down in less than five minutes. She was starving! I immediately supplemented her nursing with the bottle, but also getting up at night to nurse her and keep her with me.

Neil was irritated with her crying and my getting up to feed her. The tension between us had never gotten better since the early weeks of our marriage. "You kept me up all night when you got up and down with Amy."

I should have been able to laugh at the ludicrousness of his complaint. I used humor later to get through difficult times, but this early in my marriage, it was easier to feel nothing, to be numb. It had been a miserable time; my breasts were engorged, feeling like huge petrified grapefruits.

But, I was determined to do it right with the next one, so the first thing I did when I found out I was pregnant with Erica was to find a La Leche League meeting. When I was five months pregnant, I started attending weekly meetings and was determined to do so throughout my pregnancy. My sweet mama went with Amy and me to every meeting during the two months she was with me. Bed rest orders or no, I would not miss those La Leche meetings. La Leche League not only gave me practical tips on what to expect when breastfeeding, but also it was a little community for Amy and me.

Chapter Thirty-Four
It Won't Budge

Occasionally, my father visited us during my mother's two-month sentence in our home. One day, July 23, three days before Erica's due date, my mother glared at my stomach.

"Joe, we have to give this baby some help. Look at her belly. It's not budging." So the four of us—Mother, Pop, Amy in her stroller, and I—headed for the Missouri Botanical Gardens and we walked, it seemed, on every path in the gardens. I stopped to sit on benches along the way, but we made it. The next day, July 24, we got up and went into the kitchen, and my mother gave my belly a good thump.

"Joe! Look at it. *It's never going to drop.* Let's go home."

My parents pulled out of the driveway at about 8:30 a.m. Neil, relieved and glad to have his house and his wife back, took me in his arms, eased my bulk onto the couch and my water broke. Erica was born at noon. The state police found my parents and sent them back to St. Louis.

I am so grateful for those two years I had alone with Amy. I cherish the memory of them. It was years before our sweet intimacy was restored. I had heard it said, With every child, a mother's love is multiplied. It seemed that all my love dried up, and caring for my little ones wasn't full of love and joy but with labor, tasks, routines, charts, and exhaustion.

They were both in diapers, both were needy—Erica because I fed her on demand, and her demand was every two hours around the clock, and I provided it, along with nursing for comfort, nursing to replace a pacifier, nursing to get rid of hiccups. Amy was confused and sad. She and I had been one unit. We were never apart. Neil was gone physically or emotionally, so we had depended on each other. When Erica was born, Neil did step up to the plate to help with Amy.

"It's us against them, Amy," I heard him say. "They won't have time for us."

Footprints

Neil's words to Amy should have told me something: he was feeling ignored. Only decades later did I learn to be the wife he needed.

Life became a little easier with Erica because she was an eager nurser. But Amy and I could not get that closeness back. She seemed to withdraw from me and seek the company of other friends of mine, looking for comfort in them, not me. One day, when we were at the mall, Amy disappeared and I heard a voice over the intercom: "Will Amy Skid's mom's *friend* please come to the information table." She had requested my friend to get her, not me.

This should have been another warning. How I handled the introduction of a new baby into the family and relinquished the care of Amy to my mother had apparently offended her.

A brother offended is harder to win than a strong city (Proverbs 18:19 NKJV).

Later, Amy was far from me emotionally. I wonder how many parents who see their children recede and become distant have really offended their children and didn't recognize it. I never felt I was adequate with the girls.

If one of them was sick, I tried to find someone who was competent to take care of them, rather than myself. When they were teens, I stopped guiding them altogether, feeling like throwing up my hands. It seemed too hard.

Footprints

Years later, I was reading and there it was, glaring at me:

Listen, my son, to your father's instruction and do not forsake your mother's teaching (Proverbs 1:8 NIV).

The book dropped out of my hand. I wasn't teaching my children anything!

Conviction hit and things changed. Was it too late?

Neil still wasn't working steadily, and money became more and more scarce. Someone told me about a job that opened up just for the summer, three hours in the mornings, at Marygrove School for Wayward Girls run by the nuns. I was hired to teach French!

Chapter Thirty-Five
Me, In the Convent

The principal was Sister Gertrude, and the entire school was on lovely convent grounds. Under the direction of the nuns, it ran like clockwork. Those girls were beautifully behaved. Marygrove was a great place to work because all of the discipline was handled by the nuns. The girls told me that if they misbehaved, they would have to sleep in the laundry room.

Some of the girls at Marygrove were placed there by parents who had run out of ideas on how to get their girls to comply with family and school rules. Some were placed by the court. Girls were in Marygrove for everything from drug use to running away, law breaking, promiscuity, and incorrigibility. Most of the girls who were considered impossible outside the walls became compliant and lovely with the safe rules, the consistency, and the healthy food.

"Un flambeau, Jeanette, Isabella," was fun to sing, but I didn't know if it was appropriate to sing a religious song. After all, the song was about Jesus in the manger and Mary, his mother.

"Sister Gertrude, is it okay if I teach the girls a song about Mary?"

"Mary? Mary the mother of Jesus?" she asked.

"Yes, but it's a really nice song, and I think the girls would like singing it."

Sister Gertrude held her jiggling middle as she laughed, then held out her arm to me and placed it around my shoulder.

"Yes, Cheryl. It is perfectly okay to teach the girls a song about Mary in a convent."

She continued to chuckle long after I left to go back to my classroom.

I loved those girls and became comfortable with them and would occasionally tell them life-stories when something prompted me from the girls' own actions and conversations. I walked into class one day, and the beautiful girl had scratched her arms terribly with a tool. I decided to use that to tell them another of the many stories I shared with them about Israel.

"I spent most of my time with the Israelis who had emigrated from North Africa. They were poor and less educated than the Israelis who came from Europe. Did you read about Europe? What Hitler did to the Jews? They were put in concentration camps or killed in ovens—even little children! So when the European Jews came to Israel, they had been used to horrible situations. But, not the North Africans who I taught and who lived in my neighborhood. When the Six-Day War broke out, those Israelis from North Africa wailed and cried loudly when they heard the terrible news that their sons had been killed. They clawed their faces with their fingernails. Mothers, whose sons had been killed, were identifiable by the awful claw-marks down their cheeks."

I came to work the next day, and a beautiful girl had clawed her own face. Was I stupid? Careless? What was I thinking to give her an idea like that! I never thought she would do that. I don't think I was aware of the fragility of those girls.

By now, I had a great relationship with the girls, and I did not want to shake whatever faith they had by telling them I was Jewish. I thought that if they liked me, they would want my faith, and I wouldn't want to cause them to question their Catholic faith.

My one previous experience with the Catholic Church was St. Stanislaus in Michigan City, where my Polish babysitter had taken me to mass when I was six years old. I did not attend any of the services at Marygrove, but one day, we received a visitor. It was a priest named Father Kenneth Roberts. The girls' reaction to the priest blew me away. Father Roberts' interaction with the girls was friendly, open, and welcoming, and the girls were *joyfully* engaged during his presentation. These had been girls hardened by life, but the presence of

Father Roberts lit them from within. No, I needn't have worried about stealing the girls' faith by telling them I was Jewish. They were engaged in their faith, perhaps because of Father Roberts.

For the first time, I saw faith that was alive with love. Those girls saw something within Father Roberts that was beyond the man. They saw the God inside him. I didn't understand it then. But, I knew something important was transpiring.

Money was really tight for us, and I desperately needed to keep working. I begged, yes *begged,* Sister Gertrude to hire me for the fall semester, but she could not. She was able to hire me for the summer, but because I wasn't certified in Missouri to teach, she could not extend my position. I called the Department of Secondary and Elementary Education and asked what it would take to get Missouri Teaching Certification. One class. That was all.

Public Law 94-142 (Education for All Handicapped Children Act) passed in 1975, so all teachers were required to take a class on how to meet the needs of all students with disabilities who might be in their classes. I signed up for the required class, which was on Tuesday and Thursday evenings.

Two little girls, so little money, and no prospect of employment . . .

One day, I got a call from McCluer High School. One of their teachers, a greatly beloved French teacher, Mr. Barry, was dying of cancer. They needed someone for just one semester until they could hire a teacher. The assignment was to teach French 1–4. *One through four*. I had never taught anything past second year French, but I went in for the interview. I took a seat in the office and started to gather my thoughts about how in the world I would teach upper level French classes when my own was—well, let's put it this way: at Indiana University when we spoke French, mine always got a few laughs. I was a creative French speaker.

So, I was sitting there figuring out what I was going to say, when the administrator popped in.

"Hello, Mrs. Skid. Are you ready?"

"Well, actually, I was gathering my thoughts."

"Well, stop gathering. No need. We want you with your thoughts not gathered."

I went in and answered their questions and was told I would start teaching French 1–4 at the beginning of the fall semester, which was in eight days. I asked for copies of all the textbooks and went home to *study*. That entire semester, I studied like mad every night to stay one step ahead of the students, but I did it.

One fall day, I went into the office and took a seat to chat with the secretaries. It was the week of Standardized Testing and all the core teachers were participating, but, since I taught foreign language, I was not involved. The art teacher walked in and took a seat beside me. In his hands was a piece of sculpture he had created. I love art, so I asked about it.

Footprints

Well, this wasn't just the footprint. It was the whole foot.
The time had come. The stage was set. The props were in place.
The curtain was ready to open.

"Oh, this is something I did for the art show, but if you like art, come on down to my classroom. I would love for you to see the students' work. I'm really proud of them."

I followed Fraser Leonard downstairs to his large art room. Immediately, I was struck by a wall of paintings that were all similar. In each was a field, a fence made of rough-hewn tree branches and barbed wire. Pastels painted the expanse of skies with hope.

"Oh! I love the pastel skies," I breathed.

"Cheryl, three years ago I found the Lord Jesus Christ as my Savior. My wife and I were fighting, but Jesus healed our marriage. Our finances were rock bottom, but Jesus came in and supplied. Cheryl, my house was filled with demons that would howl and scream, but the name of Jesus sent them running."

I didn't realize it until this moment, but Fraser could have been describing our home.

I felt awkward, but didn't know how I could gracefully escape. I had no class to go to, no excuse for leaving, so I waited for an opening in his monologue. As he went on with his stories of destruction restored by "*His Savior,*" I tried looking pointedly at my watch, but he was on a roll.

He suddenly brightened and changed tactics. "Cheryl. Say this. Repeat this after me, 'Greater is He that is in me than He that is in the world.'"

To bring a quick end to this bizarre social moment, I did.

"Again! Do it again!" he repeated three times.

I wondered if the administration knew Fraser talked about that kind of stuff in a public school.

 *Fingerpointer* 

Frantic, the enemy did his best to make Fraser look outrageous and for me to discount what he was saying.

I finally got out of there, but before I left, I made an appointment for my husband and me to go to his house that night to purchase a piece of art like one I saw on the wall. Once back in the office, I checked my mailbox and picked up a few papers.

Before leaving, I turned to one of the secretaries, "Fraser was down there talking about Jesus."

She brightened. "Praise God!"

I looked toward the other, more introverted secretary.

"Fraser was down there talking about Jesus," I said.

She broke into a smile. "Glory to God."

Footprints

Stay. Connect.

The Holy Spirit connects, and the enemy of our soul divides and isolates. The believer in Jesus finds that friends are everywhere. Hearts open, and hearts connect.

With your blood you purchased for God persons from every tribe and language and people and nation (Revelation 5:9 NIV).

Such a wonderful multihued, multilingual beautiful bouquet are God's people, if only I had eyes to recognize and a heart to appreciate them.

In bounced a young African American social worker. I made eye contact. "Fraser Leonard was talking about Jesus downstairs."

Without missing a bounce, the social worker touched his forehead with his fingers. "Cool dude."

I turned, walked down the hallway, dug my car keys out of my purse, and thought, *The whole bunch is nuts. This needs to be reported. I'll make a phone call when I get home.*

I got into my car and drove out the Washington exit and turned right onto Derhake Street. I drove two blocks and was passing under a bower of trees and suddenly a presence filled my passenger seat and spoke to me . . .

"Cheryl. I Am who they say I Am. I Am the Son of God."

I knew who it was. *I knew who He was*. This Presence, this *majesty,* this *glory* taking up space and weighing down the passenger seat of my 1970 Chevy Caprice was Jesus Christ, the Son of Glory, the Lord of heaven and earth, the First and the Last, the Alpha and the Omega. Oh, ohohohohoh! I was undone. Did I know those terms? No, I did not. But there He was, and now He was putting on a technical display. I saw the whole of my life as I denied Him over and over again, but it was no longer the prints of His feet. It was if I was being held against His heart and He held me in his arms as I drove that car! I sobbed against Him.

As I drove, drowning in tears and the deepest sorrow I've ever known before or since, Jesus set before me a film strip of scenes where I'd said "no" to Him. After each one was a dreadful click as if to say, "I held you accountable."

There was the scene in my bedroom as a child when I had gone to Vacation Bible School with a friend and came home singing, "Jesus Loves Me." My mother said, "Jewish girls don't sing that song." *Click.*

But, there in my bed alone, maybe six years old, I held my arms up to Daddy God for a hug after my prayers, and I said in my heart, *What if Jesus really is Your Son?* I quickly shook my head and said to myself, "No! Jewish girls don't believe that." *Click.*

The time we went to see *Ben Hur* in Chicago with our religious school class. I saw the scene with Jesus and the woman and how her eyes lifted to Him and His eyes poured into hers. I felt an intake of breath. "If only I could believe that! But Jewish girls don't believe that." *Click.* (Now, I know that *I was the woman*, and His eyes were pouring into mine.)

The time at Indiana University when I saw a school newspaper. "Jesus loves the Jews. For more information call this number." I had picked up the phone.

"This ad says Jesus loves the Jews. Is that true? My friend wants to know."

There was just a slight pause and then the sweetest male voice I ever heard, "Dear, are you Jewish?"

"No!" I snapped and hung up. *Click.*

The semester after I came back from Israel and was living back in the dormitory and couldn't help noticing two girls down the hall who were continually talking about the Holy Spirit.

"Oh, you know when the Spirit comes," they'd say to each other as if it were an inside secret. They talked about the Holy Spirit, all rapturous, as if it were some mysterious friend that only they knew. They invited me to their Pentecostal church and, as a fun thing to do, three of us said we'd go for laughs. As we walked up to the door of the church, the preacher looked at me with respect, extended his hand, and looked in my eyes. "I understand you're Jewish. We have so much in common with you Jewish people."

I lowered my gaze and let go of his hand. Inside I had snarled, *"You have nothing in common with me." Click.*

We entered the church, and I saw ugly women with weird hairdos quietly weeping, kneeling before pews. Later, many years later, I realized that those dear and beautiful women knew I was coming, and they were weeping *for me*. As we stood with the congregation, the preacher spoke and looked directly at me, "The baptism tub is clean. Come on up." I couldn't get out of that church fast enough. *Click.*

After school was out for the summer, I had gone with some girls to the Indiana state fair. A woman was handing out small black Bibles. She extended one to me.

"Oh, no. Thanks," I said. "I'm Jewish." That had always worked for the Jehovah Witnesses who had come to my door, but she took a step toward me and smiled confidently, "Oh, dear. This Bible is *for* the Jews."

I thanked her, took it, turned the corner, and threw it in the trash. *Click.*

He was relentless. *Clickclickclickclickclickclickclick.* Denial after denial after denial. All the times I had said no to Him, yet here He was, in His glory, sitting next to me, loving me, giving me purpose, giving me reason for living, giving me hope beyond anything I'd ever known—hope and purpose I didn't even know I was missing.

"Jesus, I am so sorry! I didn't know! I don't even know who You are, but I'm following You the rest of my life."

As I said that, I felt as if metal gates were closing behind me that would never again open. For a split second, I thought of the tradition, the Judaism, the four thousand years of my people from which I was pulling—tearing—away, but *He* was there! *He* was there! *He is!*

The tears never stopped as I made my way home. I don't even know when He left my car.

Years later, I wondered if maybe it was an angel.

To which He said, "No! It was I."

And the teacher who I thought was a crazy fanatic? Jesus, Himself, confirmed Fraser Leonard's words.

Imagine! There was Fraser Leonard, an art teacher, preaching everywhere, telling me about Jesus and less than an hour later, Jesus Himself showed up in my car. How God honored the words and the heart of Fraser Leonard. He chose him for such an assignment.

And they went forth, and preached everywhere, the Lord working with them, and confirming the word with signs following (Mark 16:20 KJV).

Chapter Thirty-Six
Who, What Am I?

Finally, I reached my home. I stopped the car and just sat there, dazed, my head resting on the steering wheel. Who am I? What am I?

At last, I picked up my purse and school bags, opened the car door, and walked into my house. I dropped everything onto the couch, opened the closet, and reached for the big St. Louis Yellow Pages. *Where do I even look?* Jewish? Churches? I knew there would be nothing to fit the complexion of whom I had just become.

I scanned the names of churches and said to myself, "Baptist! That's a real church." I had heard of other denominations throughout my life, but Baptist sounded true and solid. I called three Baptist churches and each secretary heard me, in between sobs, "Hello, my name is Cheryl. I am Jewish. Jesus came in my car this afternoon, and I turned my life over to Him."

Each one said something like, "Pastor's not in. He will not be in until Tuesday. Please call back then."

Can you imagine saying that to someone who was crying and uttering those words? (If this book does nothing else, I hope it encourages people to have discerning men and women answer the phones, who will treat each caller as a true seeker and each call as vitally important.)

I kept looking. *Here was something.* Prayer Line.

I called the number and a recording said, "You have just walked through gates that have closed behind you and you're never going back that way again."

That described me!

Then the voice said, "For more information call Prince of Peace Unity Christian Church."

I did.

The pastor actually answered the phone. I told him the whole story ending with, "I want to come to your church!"

He paused. "Cheryl, you are welcome, but you don't belong here. We believe all roads lead to God. You have had a fundamental Christian experience."

At the time I didn't know what he meant. He meant, by fundamental Christian experience, I was like a person in the biblical accounts. They saw Jesus, and knowing who He was, they fell at His feet and worshiped Him alone. The fundamental Christian takes the Bible at its Word.

Maybe the fundamental church would have been like the Baptist churches I had called.

Pastor O was letting me know that in Unity all roads lead to God. Jesus is one way of many. All I knew at the time was that he had voiced my longing, and I had to get there. Interestingly, since that first time I called the church many times and can count on two fingers the number of times he answered.

"I believe all roads lead to God!" I was wailing, pleading. He told me the time of their service and gave me directions to the church, and I made plans to go that Sunday.

In summary, Fraser told me his story about Jesus in his house.

That led to me going to my car disgusted with him for sharing his faith openly in school, and then Jesus came into my car to prove His words.

Fraser didn't attempt to disciple me at all.

Later, as I studied the Word and learned the importance of discipleship, I wondered about Fraser—just leaving me there. But you can see I didn't stay there.

One sows, another waters, and God makes it grow.

It's not important who does the planting, or who does the watering. What's important is that God makes the seed grow (1 Corinthians 3:7 NLT).

The next day after my morning class, I walked with the Jewish Spanish teacher to the teacher's lounge where we sat together with a room full of teachers for lunch. Suddenly, Fraser walked to the door.

His tall frame filled the door, and he pointed his finger at me and boomed, "Just look at her! You can see Jesus Christ all over her face!"

The Jewish Spanish teacher next to me said, "Shut up, Fraser. You're nuts. You're Jewish, aren't you, Cheryl?"

I meekly answered, "Yes."

Footprints

I denied Fraser's words because of the peer pressure of the woman next to me, and that was serious business. The Bible is very stern about pretending not to know God while we are here on earth and can make an impact.

"But everyone who denies me here on earth, I will also deny before my Father in heaven" (Matthew 10:33 NLT).

Thank God! He gave me so many second chances.

I had not driven on a highway in St. Louis and was terrified of the traffic. I got lost a few times on the way to Unity Church and arrived an hour late, well into the service.

Footprints

That was my first opportunity to overcome my fear in pursuing Jesus. I had been terrified of highway driving, but I was more intent to get where Jesus was than to crumble under my fear.

For God has not given us a spirit of fear, but of power and of love and of a sound mind (2 Timothy 1:7 NKJV).

After that first time, I started to attend the Unity Church regularly. How did Neil feel about this? Well, when I told him what I had done, what had happened to me in the car, he had said, "You'll get over it. Something like this happened to me once, but I'm Jewish and not giving it up. You'll get over it."

But I didn't "get over it." Recently, Neil confessed that when he heard what I had done, he set out to make my life miserable.

One day, a vacuum cleaner salesman came to the door and asked if he could show us the Kirby vacuum cleaner. He did. He came in, showed us the Kirby, and we bought it. (That was in 1978, and it still works today.) Before he left, he brought up faith and started to tell me about Jesus. I told him that I had accepted Jesus as Savior and was going to the Unity Church.

"Ma'am. That is a cult. You need to get out."

"Oh, that's ridiculous. They're very nice."

After we bought the vacuum cleaner, he offered to come back the next week with some literature about Unity. He was true to his word. Not only did he bring me information about Unity but also he invited Neil to accompany him as his guest to a Full Gospel Businessmen's breakfast.

Neil went with him and came home, saying, "Whatever those men have, they really believe it!" We can see the obvious footprint of the Lord here, standing right beside the vacuum salesman.

I decided I needed a New Testament, so I went to some garage sales and bought a paperback version of *Good News for Modern Man* for ten cents. I started the habit of reading it every day and calling the Unity pastor to tell him what I learned. He seldom answered my calls, so I left messages. But something was troubling me. I read the Bible and compared it with what I was learning at the Unity Church, and it didn't match.

Footprints

And the people of Berea were more open-minded than those in Thessalonica, and they listened eagerly to Paul's message. They searched the Scriptures day after day to see if Paul and Silas were teaching the truth (Acts 17:11 NLT).

Without realizing it, I was searching the Scriptures daily, and I was checking with the messages at the Unity Church against the Word of Truth.

I invited the pastor to come to dinner, and he agreed. I had everything made and on the table when he called and said something had come up. He wasn't coming. How strange!

I considered the reasons he may have cancelled at the last minute. Fear of confronting an angry husband? The realization that I was seeing truth in the Bible that I wasn't seeing at Unity and not wanting to confront his own doubts?

I decided Unity wasn't the church for me. I told the secretaries at school about my concerns with the Unity Church, how what I was hearing there didn't fit with what I was reading daily in my Bible. One of the school secretaries invited me to her Nazarene church. I accepted her invitation and went the following Sunday.

I walked in and sat down. In front of me was a woman in a sundress who was weeping. I found out that her daughter had cancer and the church had taken up a collection to send her to Chicago where she would get a special hypothermia treatment in hopes of stopping the growth of the disease.

When I saw the love and commitment of this church toward a single mom fighting such a battle I thought, *This is the real church.*

Instead of footprints, the Lord was nudging me through what we call an "inward witness," a knowing. When I sat in the Nazarene Church and saw the love they had for one another, my inward witness—my "gut," my spirit—said, "Yes. This is it."

I called the pastor of Unity and told him I didn't see cohesiveness between what I read in the Bible and what I heard in the pulpit or saw in the people at Unity, and so I had left to attend a church I believed was closer to the Bible in its beliefs.

Two years later, I called to check on that pastor. "Oh, he has left the church," I was told. "He was born again. Half of the church members left at the same time."

Maybe the Spirit of the Lord inside me was strong, and the pastor recognized it and ran after the Lord. That's a blessing.

That experience was the beginning of "signs following" in my life where the Lord would confirm His Word—putting a stamp of approval on what I was doing, as He had done with Fraser Leonard's testimony followed by Jesus' appearance in my car. It was a new way of communicating to me, through me—an honor and a blessing.

Chapter Thirty-Seven

Getting Used to My New Identity

At the Nazarene church, I felt like the Jew-on-Call. It was as if they expected me to be an expert on Judaism. Actually, I learned that's pretty common with how Gentile Christians view Jews—as experts in the Old Testament and tradition. Neil and I were asked to present a Seder, which we did, even though Neil was antagonistic about my relationship with Jesus and the church. I was asked to serve on a panel on the Second Coming.

"The Second Coming? I just heard about the first one. There's another?"

Pastor Daniel knew that it was just a matter of time until Jews would come in—a marvelous ingathering, at the right time—to take their rightful place as branches. Pastor Daniel knew what many, sadly, do not know—that God is far from done with the Jews; in fact, they are still the apple of His eye.

Footprints

After a period of glory, the LORD of Heaven's Armies sent me against the nations who plundered you. For he said, "Anyone who harms you harms my most precious possession" (Zechariah 2:8 NLT).

I was asked about my feelings about submission to the husband.

"You've got to be kidding. Submit? Crazy! Jewish women are *anything* but submissive to their husbands. We rule the roost."

Pastor Daniel was so incredibly patient and understanding with me—not only patient but also respectful of the Judaism which I was bringing to his church. He loved it!

He caught the importance the Lord put on the Jews believing. They were the first to whom evangelists were to go—to the Jew first. I was actually the first Jewish person Pastor Daniel knew who turned to Jesus, and he was awed by the metamorphosis as Jesus gained more and more of my heart. It blessed him so much!

But his question about submission made me realize that I needed to study what it meant to be a Christian woman. I had "Jewish woman" down pat. In my Jewish community, a woman got married, got a cleaning lady and a babysitter, pursued a career, and gave back to the community.

Christianity was a new way of living. I studied these Christian women. They cared about each other, taking casseroles when women were sick. That wasn't different from Sinai Temple. My mother always had a casserole or a cake ready to take to someone, even if she didn't know them.

Here's an example of my mother's heart of service: My mother, father, brother, and I were fishing on the pier when the man next to us had a heart attack. Someone notified the paramedics. They arrived at the pier and made their way down to where we stood. Before his wife followed in their automobile, my mother asked for her phone number. Then she fixed meals, took them over to their home, and kept up with them, making sure the family had food until her husband was out of the woods.

Another example—yes, I love bragging about my mother: a little girl was in the hospital when my pop was in for surgery. My mother took her knitting and reading materials to my father's room, but she always popped into the little girl's room. She noticed that the small child never had a visitor, so she brought gifts and played with her. After my pop was released from the hospital, my mother continued visiting the little girl every day until the child died.

So, I was very used to women caring and serving. But what set these women apart?

I learned the difference wasn't in what they *did,* but in whose they were.

Ephesians 2:8 says that it is not what we *do* that leads to our salvation, but simply a belief in who Jesus is and an overwhelming desire to belong to Him and to please Him.

Jesus told them, "This is the only work God wants from you: Believe in the one he has sent" (John 6:29 NLT).

I learned through the years that God doesn't want results from us; He wants belief in Him. Only. We love Jesus! We believe in Jesus! That is all He wants. When we go out to share the Word of God, that person's salvation is not the result for which God looks. After all, He is the one who produces that result in the person's heart. It is by the Holy Spirit that we have faith to believe.

I became very close with Pastor Daniel and his wife and spent hours in their lovely home. I took Amy and Erica over, and they would destroy their home, flinging toys everywhere.

Footprints

Pastor Daniel's wife was patient. "No. Don't bother cleaning it up. It'll take me five minutes."

But the fruit of the Spirit is love, joy, peace, patience, kindness, goodness, faith, gentleness, self-control. Against such things there is no law (Galatians 5:22–23 HCBS).

Oh, now here was something I needed! Patience. I learned about the fruit of the spirit and have spent a lifetime creating an environment in my own heart in which it could grow.

Chapter Thirty-Eight

Neil Fights Back Using Jewish Marriage Encounter

The church members were very kind to Neil and invited us to events that did not revolve around Jesus. People tiptoed around him because of his fury about my love for Jesus. They didn't mention Jesus, or even God.

Pastor Dan did give us a record album with biblical songs. "Neil, these are all songs from your Bible, the Old Testament," he said.

At the time, I thought Pastor Dan was placating Neil, but through the years, and especially now, in reflection—seeing things through the veil of time—I realize that Pastor Dan had such a reverence for Judaism that he didn't just choose the songs for Neil but for himself.

Neil seemed to enjoy their company, although it was hard to tell. He said little, and at events in their homes he often lay down in the middle of the floor and fell asleep. But he always agreed to go when I said, "We're invited to a party (or hayride or dinner) at the home of someone from Trinity."

Footprints

The Lord is so impressed with hospitality.

Do not forget to show hospitality to strangers, for by so doing some people have shown hospitality to angels without knowing it (Hebrews 13:2 NIV).

Neil was no angel but definitely a stranger to the kingdom. Oh! Hospitality! I can't stress it enough!

But his blood boiled when the girls and I went to church on Sunday mornings. He will readily tell you that part of his plan to make my life miserable was to berate me about spending time in church. There were midweek services on Wednesdays and another service on Sunday evenings, but I only went one time a week. When I did eventually join a women's group, I made sure it was during the day when he was gone so it wouldn't interfere with my time with him.

Maybe submission to my husband was starting without my knowing it. I never, ever knowingly tried to submit to or obey my husband. It was happening, as in the days before I knew Jesus, He taught me of Himself through the spirit on the inside of me which would one day explode into a knowing of His wonderful Self!

Then came summer, and a young lady asked if she and her sister could take my girls to a Child Evangelism Fellowship backyard Bible Club every day for one week. One of the sisters had been in my class the day after Jesus appeared in my car and had heard the whole story—no details omitted.

Did I find it odd that the day after I had been on my way to report a teacher for talking about Jesus, I told—in detail—each of my classes what happened to me in my car? Of all the students, this young lady, Cheryl Bryant, had been the only one who stepped up to tell me she shared my faith. She was full of joy for me and gave me a Christmas mug—"Jesus is the Reason for the Season"—with a note saying, "This Christmas will mean so much to you." That had created a special bond between us.

Of course, I was delighted that she and her sister, Andrea, wanted to take my girls every morning for the week to show them a special time and to teach them about Jesus.

One evening Neil had *had* it. That day, Andrea and I went to the backyard Bible club and took Amy and Erica. At supper, they started to belt out a song they learned that day. "Jesus died for sinful men, and one day, He'll come again to take us all to *heaven*!"

"No more. No more! If you want to go to that church go, but you don't poison my kids!"

I didn't put up a fuss or argue. I left the girls home and went to church alone.

At the same time I was going to church, learning more about Jesus, Neil was on a crusade of his own to drag me back into the fold, which he thought I'd left. I say he *thought* I left, but of course I hadn't. Remember, Jesus came for the Jew first.

In fact, while I was at church, Neil would sit down with one of the rabbis at the synagogue. Neil was getting more and more and more "Jewish" in the sense of traditions and paraphernalia. Finally, he came home with a brochure for Jewish Marriage Encounter.

"Let's go to this," he said. "It will be good for our marriage." The brochure said something about falling in love again. Well, we had never been that much in love in the beginning, so going back to that first love would not be fireworks. But he wanted to go.

The first thing I had to do was to wean Erica. At twenty-two months, she was still nursing, which is not at all unusual in La Leche League (still every two hours around the clock, I might add, which was my fault, not hers, as she continues to remind me). So what to do?

Every week, we got fresh eggs and chickens from Mr. Rhemer who lived in Illinois and dropped them off at our house. So the week Neil brought home the brochure and after the "egg man" came by, Erica walked up to me and said, "Boosie?" This was her word for bosom or "time to nurse me."

"Oh, honey, the egg man's wife had a baby and I had to give it to her." And that was weaning. I called a friend to see if she could watch Amy and Erica while we went to Jewish Marriage Encounter.

Neil and I drove to the hotel and checked in. I went reluctantly. Our marriage hurt me more than it soothed me, and I didn't want to feel all the pain I knew would accompany having to concentrate on our life together. I went into the first session with my jaw locked in resistance. It took less than ten minutes for my tears to start—tears that had been blocked. The pain that was buried surfaced and flowed out through my eyes. Something inside me was broken and rivers started flowing.

From there, we went to do our first of many communication assignments, and we shared our hearts as we never had before. The brochure had said, "Fall in love like you were when you got married." I never felt loved in the marriage. Now, for the first time, I found myself softening toward Neil. As I loved him more, I was aware of Jesus less.

Neil took advantage of that new submissive attitude he saw in me. Now was the time he could convince me that church was no place for a nice Jewish wife.

 *Fingerpointer* 

How could this be? Obviously God wanted us to love each other. But to love Jesus less in the process? I didn't realize that Exodus 20:3—*"Thou shalt have no other gods before me,"* as I learned in Sinai Temple Sunday school in third grade—could mean husbands. God is so good to give us multiple chances to get it right.

God later goes on to say in Matthew 19:29 (NLT), "And everyone who has given up houses or brothers or sisters or father or mother or children or property, for my sake, will receive a hundred times as much in return and will inherit eternal life."

We are continually tested to see if we are "willing to let that go for Me?"

Would God do that with a spouse? Read the text. But at the time I had not read that at all. All I knew is that I was falling more in love with Neil, while Jesus, Bible, and church were slipping away. Technicolor was becoming black and white, and fading.

Those days were like a honeymoon. Perhaps Neil saw my love for him and felt that the time was right.

"Cheryl. You make a choice. You can be Christian or you can be Jewish. You can't be both. Pick one. You either go to synagogue with me or to church without me. Not both." We had been going to synagogue every Saturday as a family, and I had been going to church alone on Sunday.

I didn't know then what I know now: Jesus came for the Jews first. Jesus was Jewish. Matthew was Jewish. Mark was Jewish. John was Jewish. Paul was Jewish. Stephen was Jewish. The groups that worshiped, celebrated, and followed the teachings of Jesus in those early days of the church did not meet in a fancy building with stained glass, a steeple, a statue of Jesus, or a cross. The church was a group of people who, out of their free will, were called out together with others of like mind for a purpose—to worship Jesus Christ as Savior and to learn everything they could about living like Him.

All I knew was that Jesus appeared in my car, filling my passenger seat with Himself. He spoke to me. He *really* was the Son of God. I decided in that split-second that following Him was worth giving up everything. Satan saw his opportunity, and he grabbed it. And I fell for it.

"Neil. No problem. You're my husband. I'll go with you to synagogue and stay home from church. But if we don't go to synagogue one Saturday, I'll go to church on Sunday because I need something spiritual every week." So, for a year, I was out of church.

One afternoon, after being out of church a few months, I scratched my eye with a comb. The pain was so awful that I had to keep my eye closed; then if I tried to open it, all I saw was brown. I went to bed that night, and when I woke in the middle of the night, it was worse.

"Neil! It hurts. I can't even open it at all now."

"I wish you had told me this earlier," he grumbled getting out of bed and into his clothes. We called a neighbor to stay with the girls and started to leave for the emergency

"Wait! My Bible."

"Ridiculous! That is the last thing you need." He snorted. "Just get in the car."

But I insisted and ran back for my big, red copy of *The Open Bible*. All the way to the ER, I moaned and cried about the pain in my eye, which was now filled with gummy brown goo. The pain was like sharp knives.

But as I entered the waiting room and sat down, I looked at my Bible. It was as if I came to my senses: I shouldn't be whining and acting so defeated.

"I am an ambassador of Christ," I said aloud. That fast, my eye cleared up, and everything was totally clear.

Just then, an intern with sleep-messy hair came around the corner. He glanced at the chart and at me. "What have we here?"

Brightly, I told him, "My eye was sealed shut with goo because I scratched it and the pain was unbearable, but when I looked at my Bible and said, 'I am an ambassador of Christ,' Jesus healed my eye."

He stopped and stared. "Well, in case your healing goes away, here is a patch." And he gave me instructions on how to use it.

I was still out of church, holding fast to the commitment I had made to Neil to go with him to synagogue and not go to church. But Easter was approaching.

"Neil, may I please go to church on Easter?"

"You ain't going anywhere near a church on Easter," he snapped, not looking at me. The tender love he seemed to have for me, which had precipitated the "ultimatum," was gone.

Early Easter morning, while it was still dark, Neil woke up with horrendous pain. He had a history of kidney stones and knew what it was.

"I have to go to the hospital." He quickly packed a bag and we got into the car. Nurses and doctors came into the room to which he'd been assigned. They hooked him up to an IV, and I stood next to him as he lay in his bed. The hospital staff waited to see if the kidney stone would pass. But I kept my eye on the clock.

If I left right then, I could get to the Nazarene church just in time for my favorite part—the altar call.

At the end of each service, Pastor Dan called on everyone who had a need or a praise to come forward. When church was a regular routine for me, I was on my knees at the altar every week. How could people not have one or the other—a praise or a need?

So I left the hospital, jumped into the car, drove to church, parked, ran inside, flew down the aisle, and threw myself onto the altar in my jeans and strawberry T-shirt, just in time.

Today, it is not unusual for people to go to some church facilities wearing any old thing, but at that time in the Nazarene church, men dressed in suits and women in ladylike garments. I knelt and poured out my heart to God. Afterward I rose, left, and went back to the hospital. Neil passed the stone the next day.

Carol, the pastor's wife, was troubled about the length of my being out of fellowship. "Cheryl I'm concerned about your salvation."

I told her she had nothing to worry about.

Now, I realize that there was definitely cause for concern.

 *Fingerpointer* 

Separating from the body of Christ, from teaching, is a way to grow cold, like the proverbial piece of coal that's been removed from the pile of burning embers. Left alone, it will eventually stop burning. In fact there is a Scripture that says, "He that endureth to the end shall be saved" (Matt 10:22 KJV).

That implies there are snares, traps, and decisions that can cause a break in the path.

We always have a choice. Always! The word endure implies that the one on the path keeps going until the end, no matter what. But I had made a commitment to Neil, and I had total peace about it. I would never recommend this or anything else I have done in my walk before or after my coming to Christ. But, it is the truth of what I did, and there must be some reason I am sharing it with you.

Neil became more and more enmeshed in Judaism, not only going to synagogue on Saturday mornings, but also making appointments with the rabbi on additional days. One comment the rabbi made was interesting. "Don't worry, Neil. Their second coming will be our first coming."

What that said to me was that he knew who Jesus was, but he wasn't ready to acknowledge it. He would wait for the second chance. Why else would he say that? Their second—our first—has to be an acknowledgment that it is the same Person.

That's a chance I do not suggest anyone take.

Footprints

Today, if you hear His voice, do not harden your hearts as you did in the rebellion (Hebrews 3:15 NIV).

"You'll get over it," Neil had told me. "I did that years ago, and I got over it." What he was referring to was the time a monk told him about Jesus. Neil thought about his family, his tradition, and what he would lose, and he hardened his heart. In Matthew, we see a young man talking to Jesus as Neil had been talking to the monk. Like the young man, Neil asked, "How can I have this?"

Jesus said to him, "If you want to be perfect, go, sell what you have and give to the poor, and you will have treasure in heaven; and come, follow Me."

But when the young man heard that saying, he went away sorrowful, for he had great possessions (Matthew 19:21–22 NKJV).

For the rich young man, "all he had" to give away was great wealth.

For Neil, it was family, tradition, and "will they disown me?"

Both walked away.

After Jewish Marriage Encounter, we were encouraged to continue practicing the wonderful principles we learned. They divided us into groups, which would become little families meeting once a month. We met the first time and someone suggested we call ours The Love Family. It was fabulous. Couples took turns presenting each month, and the love poured out of all of us as we heard each couple share the pain and the healing that started with Jewish Marriage Encounter. It was cleansing to share deep heart issues. The time came for Neil and me to share our journey, and everyone rushed up to us afterwards with tears streaming down their cheeks.

The one thing I did not share was what happened to me in the car the day that Jesus overwhelmed me with Himself.

Why? Was I afraid they would not accept me? Was I ashamed? That is no small thing.

 Footprints 

Luke 9:26 (ESV) can't be clearer on this subject: *"For whoever is ashamed of me and of my words, of him will the Son of Man be ashamed when he comes in his glory and the glory of the Father and of the holy angels."*

I am so glad for multiple second chances! I would hate for anyone ever to think she has made a mistake after salvation that would put her back to "Start Over."

I learned once, from my time with the Lord, that when a man or woman of God falls—no matter how hard—repents, and pours out love to God in true sorrow, they don't go back to the beginning. They go back to where they fell off the track. Hopefully, that will give someone huge relief.

Get back on track!

This is a small, trivial example, but did you ever have an armload of library books that are so overdue it would cost the week's grocery money to pay the fine? Then one day, there is the library fine amnesty.

"Bring the books back with a can of food, and your fine is erased."

Jesus' forgiveness is always available. Never a "get back to the back of the line." But, "Hop back on. Get back in the game. You're Mine! I've been watching you. My eyes never left you once!"

Jewish Marriage Encounter had Neil's intended effect on me. My love for Neil and the group grew, and my zeal for Jesus waned. The entire group met a considerable distance from us, and there really were no Jewish people we knew in our section of St. Louis County.

One day, Neil said he met a Jewish guy at work, and he and his Jewish wife would like to get together with us. So, we met the one Jewish couple besides us who lived in Florissant. We met often for meals at each other's house, never sharing anything other than surface, friendly conversation. I never mentioned anything about my faith. That would have enraged Neil and turned off the other couple. I knew, because before Jesus was my Savior, I saw any Jew who turned to Jesus as being a turncoat. A traitor.

One day, the wife, Sharon, and I made plans to meet just inside Jamestown Mall and walk to Sears where she had to pick up a paycheck. As we walked along the mall, we passed a Christian bookstore. I longingly glanced at it out of the corner of my eye, thinking that when Sharon and I parted, I would go back and look. But Sharon walked toward it.

"Cheryl, do you ever go in here?"

I hesitated, not wanting to give away my interest in anything Christian to this Jewish friend.

"Well, once in a long while, I may see a gift for a child in the window and go in to take a look," I said, with a shrug of nonchalance.

"Well," she said, striding toward the middle of the store, "let me tell you what I look at in here." She pointed to a large collection of Watchman Nee, one of the most radical evangelists to come out of China.

I stopped, stunned, and whispered, "Sharon, are you a Christian?"

Chapter Thirty-Nine
Jesus! He Never Lost One!

As she said, "Yes," I gave a *whoop!* and we jumped up and down, holding each other as shoppers looked on.

"I knew," she said. "You gave it away all the time without saying a word."

Apparently, without my speaking the name of Jesus or praying or doing anything else that "Christians" do to identify themselves, the Spirit of the Lord within me was communicating with the Spirit of the Lord inside Sharon. Mysteries. What an adventure to love Jesus!

Footprints

This was to fulfill the words He had said, "I have not lost one of those You have given me" (John 18:9 HCSB).

When Elizabeth heard Mary's greeting, the baby leaped in her womb, and Elizabeth was filled with the Holy Spirit (Luke 1:41 NET).

Jesus split heaven again by bringing courageous Sharon into my life when my embers were cooling. Our visits changed in focus. Instead of mundane topics, we talked about Jesus, faith, and how to grow in Christ. She mentioned a woman's name that I didn't recognize. Laverne Anderson had founded a Bible College called *Lael,* Devoted to God. Sharon told of this woman's faith, focus, and fierce loyalty to Christ. I tucked her name away.

One day, about a month later, I felt the sudden urge to pray for Neil to accept Jesus as the Son of God. I never had prayed that for him. The life of a Jewish woman in love with Jesus had been lonely. I'd cut off all my Jewish friends. I hadn't breathed a word to the Jewish Marriage Encounter Love Family. I didn't seem to fit anywhere.

Today, there are Messianic groups everywhere, but then? I didn't know of any at that time. So it was a lonely walk. Lonely and homesick. During the High Holy Days, I longed for synagogue. I missed the people, the culture, the easy communication with Jews everywhere—instant *mishpocha* (family). But I couldn't ignore that gut-unction in the car when Jesus sat down.

So now, I knelt down in my dining room and began to pray silently. *"Lord, is it okay for me to pray for Neil to accept You as his Savior?"*

I got the impression that not only was it okay for me to pray for Neil, but it was something God, Himself, was expecting, awaiting. I didn't have to say another word.

Footprints

"But you shall receive power when the Holy Spirit has come upon you; and you shall be witnesses to Me in Jerusalem, and in all Judea and Samaria, and to the end of the earth" (Acts 1:8 NKJV).

Had the Holy Ghost come upon me? All I know is that I was hit in the gut with the need to pray for Neil to be born again. It would be years hence, but I would indeed proclaim to the ends of the earth. But right now, I was alone in my dining room in St. Louis, my Jerusalem.

It was as if I were watching a movie right in front of my eyes. That's how real it was. First, I saw a stone slab . . . long and cold. Above it, I saw a cross erected and, on the cross, the body of Jesus. On the slab I saw, suddenly, Neil lying there, cold as the stone and dead. As I stared, the blood started, drop and drop and drop and drop and drop from sweet Jesus onto Neil. Into Neil, saturating him. I don't know how long I knelt there, but suddenly, it was done.

For this is my blood of the new testament, which is shed for many for the remission of sins (Matthew 26:28 KJV).

Just think—as surely as those drops saturated Neil when I watched him lying beneath the cross, just as surely did His precious blood saturate you when you cried out for His salvation, realizing that you could never do it alone.

No rules, regulations, or visits to a church can do what the Blood can do.

I knew it. He was born again! I stood up, joyous, and called Carol, the wife of the Nazarene pastor.

"It's done!" I shouted. "Neil believes that Jesus is the Son of God!" It was as if I could see Carol's beautiful face, eyes aglow toward heaven.

"What did he say?"

"Carol, he didn't say anything. He doesn't know yet. But it's done. I know it. It's done." I said nothing to Neil, but went about my days with a new lightness of heart.

Footprints

Once again, I declared what I had not yet learned from a pastor or from anyone: We must believe it in our hearts before we see it with our eyes.

And Jesus answered and said to them, "Truly, I say to you, if you have faith and do not doubt, you will not only do what was done to the fig tree, but even if you say to this mountain, 'Be taken up and cast into the sea,' it will happen.

"And all things you ask in prayer, believing, you will receive" (Matthew 21:21–22 NASB).

And had I even asked for Neil's salvation? Not really. I asked God if I could ask Him! Amazing!

Two weeks later, Neil said, "Something's missing from our home."

"What do you mean?

"Something spiritual," he snapped.

"Something spiritual is missing from our home? You have *havdala* candles (braided candles lit at the end of Shabbat), Shabbat candles. You have incense. You have a *mezuzah* on the door (parchment inscribed with part of the Torah—that is, the first five books of the Bible enclosed in a decorative case), *menorahs* (candelabras), prayer books, a prayer shawl, a *yarmulke* (skullcap). What's missing?"

"People."

I looked at him, incredulous. "People? You mean Christians?"

"Yes!" he shouted looking cross.

"Wait. You mean you're telling me that you want Christians to be in our home, yet I can't go to church?"

"Yes."

Chapter Forty

The Parade of the Saints

So began the Friday night Shabbat dinners when, one by one, we invited Christian couples from the Nazarene church for a meal.

They were all scared to death of Neil, so they would never even think of bringing up the subject of Jesus. Eventually, I ran out of couples to invite. I called Sharon.

"Hey Sharon, I want to invite Dr. Laverne Anderson to dinner."

"Forget it. She's so busy. She'll never come."

I persisted. "Sharon, at least take me to her office. Let me meet her and invite her."

"Okay. I'll pick you up tomorrow at ten. I'll give her a call to let her know we're coming."

We walked into the little office that held Lael University. Dr. LaVerne Anderson, in her mid-sixties, was a vision wearing a flowing, gauzy, lavender skirt, her black hair curling, trailing wisps all over her head and down her shoulders. I got straight to the point after a brief introduction.

"Dr. Anderson, my husband, Neil, is hard against Jesus, but he wants Christians in the house. Will you come to dinner Friday night?"

"Give me your hand," Laverne said, her piercing eyes looking steadily into mine. "Jesus, I want You to do anything you need to do to bring Cheryl's husband, Neil, to You, even if it means breaking both his legs."

I tried to pull my hand away at this dire thought, but she held firm.

"I'll be there," she said.

I was learning to believe that gut feeling that said, "Do this. Go there."

That gut feeling would be something vital to the world ministry God had waiting for me.

 *Footprints* 

Your own ears will hear him. Right behind you a voice will say, "This is the way you should go," whether to the right or to the left (Isaiah 30:21 NLT).

Friday night came. The table was set, Shabbat candles ready. The girls were scrubbed and excited about more Shabbat guests. The doorbell rang and she was at the door. I introduced Dr. Anderson to Neil and the children.

She was delightful, friendly, and laden with gifts. Her presence filled the room. There was something for everyone. The most memorable was a board game about Jesus going to the cross. Shocking! I looked at Neil for his expression and could just imagine what my parents would think on their next visit . . . Jesus going to the cross . . . a game for children. Oy!

I invited Dr. Anderson and the family to the table. All gathered 'round and found seats. I picked up a match and lit the Shabbat candles. "*Baruch Ata Adonai Eloheinu Adonai Echad Melech Ha'olam Asher Kaddishanu b' Mitzva Tov V'Tzivanu L'hadlik Ner Shel Shabbat.* (Blessed art Thou, O Lord our God, King of the Universe, who has sanctified us by Thy Law and commanded us to kindle the Sabbath lights)."

Neil picked up the wine glass, "*Baruch Atah Adonai Elohenu Melech Ha'Olam Boreh Pri Ha goffen.* (Blessed art Thou, O Lord our God, King of the Universe, who created the fruit of the vine.)" Neil picked up the bread and broke it. "*Baruch Atah Adonai Elohenu Melech Ha'olam ha Motzeh lechem min ha aretz.* (Blessed art Thou, O Lord our God, who bringest forth the bread from the earth)."

"Go ahead and start your salads. Neil, will you help me bring in the chicken?" We walked into the kitchen, and my veins turned to ice. Oh! Oh, no!

I couldn't believe it. I'd neglected to turn on the oven. Our dinner was delayed by one hour. I turned the oven to 350 degrees, and Neil and I headed, slowly, back into the dining room.

"I am so sorry," I said, returning to the table and sitting down. "I forgot to turn on the oven. We have an hour and a half before dinner is served."

Dr. Anderson was as cool as a cucumber. She reached into her large tote and brought out the *biggest* Bible I had ever seen and pulled her chair up close to Neil. I mean the Bible was *big*. It made my big red *The Open Bible* look like a miniature.

Patting Neil on the arm, she encouraged him to look where she was pointing. He glanced at me. I glanced down, but then sneaked a look at them out of the corner of my eye.

"Neil, I am going to show you every time Jesus is seen in the Old Testament. This is your Bible, the one you read and study, the one your rabbis share at synagogue. "

She turned to Genesis 1:2. "'The Spirit hovered over the deep.' Neil, the world was formless and God was speaking. While He was speaking, the Spirit was hovering. Who was the Spirit?"

Without waiting for an answer, which wasn't coming, she turned to Genesis 1:26. "'Let Us make man in Our own image.'" She looked at Neil. "Neil, that is plural. Who was with God the Father that He said, 'Let Us'?"

Then she turned to Exodus 3:2. "'There the angel of the Lord appeared to him in flames of fire from within a bush.' Neil, you know these Scriptures. I know you have studied them since you were this high," she said, holding her hand up to indicate the height of a small child.

I couldn't take my eyes off the two of them. Neil's eyes were burning into Dr. Anderson's as she spoke to him.

Then she turned to Daniel 3:25. "'Look!' Nebuchadnezzar shouted. 'I see four men unbound walking around in the fire unharmed! And the fourth looks like a god!' Neil, you know the story of Daniel. I know that your synagogue teachers taught it to you. Did they ever ask you to consider who was the fourth man in the furnace who looked like a god?"

Dr. Anderson only brought up those passages, which every Jewish child was taught in religious school. Then she changed the subject.

"Neil, your wife and children are believers in Jesus Christ. There is going to be a great rapture in which everyone believing in Jesus will be suddenly taken up to heaven, and disaster, unlike any other, will crash down on earth. The Jews will be hunted and killed, but don't worry. I have purchased land where you can hide. And here. Read this book." She handed him the book *Michael, Michael, Why Do You Hate Me?* by Michael Esses.

Footprints

The rapture is a doctrine from the Scriptures that refers to a time where the church—the believers in Jesus Christ—will all be taken up from the earth, leaving everyone else to cope.

It will happen in a moment, in the blink of an eye, when the last trumpet is blown. For when the trumpet sounds, those who have died will be raised to live forever. And we who are living will also be transformed (1 Corinthians 15:52 NLT).

For this we say unto you by the word of the Lord, that we which are alive and remain unto the coming of the Lord shall not prevent them which are asleep. For the Lord himself shall descend from heaven with a shout, with the voice of the archangel, and with the trump of God: and the dead in Christ shall rise first: then we which are alive and remain shall be caught up together with them in the clouds, to meet the Lord in the air: and so shall we ever be with the Lord (1 Thessalonians 4:15–17 KJV).

Dinner was ready.

Once dinner was served, conversation became more normal, centered around families and life in St. Louis, but my mind was buzzing. *What in the world would Neil think?*

She left, and Neil said nothing. But Tuesday, he said, "I want you to have that woman back again Friday night."

So, I called Dr. Anderson, and she agreed to return for dinner. As we were sitting down for dinner Neil spoke, his eyes fixed on Laverne.

"You see, Dr. Anderson, I have been watching these people, and they have loved me, even though I have behaved horribly. I was rude to them. I fell asleep in the middle of their living rooms. I was mean to Cheryl in front of them. They had no reason to be kind to me, but they were."

This was definitely a case of the godly behavior of people who never preached a word to Neil, winning Him over by their behavior, love, and acceptance of him.

Footprints

Your godly lives will speak to them without any words. They will be won over (1 Peter 3:1 NLT).

Neil continued. "I thought, 'God is this real? Is there really a Jesus who really is Your Son? If there isn't a Jesus who is Your Son, then I have nothing to lose by asking, and the people are all nuts.'

"Monday night I lay down in bed and said, 'God, if it is true, Jesus, if you really are who they say You are, please come and fill me with your peace and love.' Dr. Anderson, it was as if a warm honey starting at the top of my head worked its way down and filled all of me."

Chapter Forty-One

The Believing Husband Changes the Dynamics

I hadn't realized how much Neil had fought my faith until he wasn't fighting anymore. Suddenly, he was in alliance with me. The first day he walked down that aisle of Trinity Church of the Nazarene, every eye was on him. Shortly afterward, he felt the urgency to be baptized. I had never been baptized. It seemed way too over-the-top "Gentile," as had communion. But Neil was adamant that he wanted to be baptized, so I called Pastor Dan Ketchum, and he arranged for a baptism for both of us to be held at the swimming pool of a church member. Neil invited Dr. LaVerne Anderson.

Things were happening so fast. I saw that when the man takes his place in the family, God changes him quickly so that he can lead strong and well.

A few days later, two friends invited me to a Ladies Day Good News breakfast that was held one Tuesday of every month at a local church. They had invited me to go to midweek services several times before, but I thought that was nonsense. Who needs church more than once a week? But this time, it was a breakfast and they were paying, so I said I would go.

We arrived, got our breakfasts, and prepared to hear the speaker, Bob Gass, from Scotland. His message was on the scarlet thread that Rahab hung from the window. At the end of the message he said, "If anyone wants to be born again, stand up and say this prayer with me." I closed my eyes (probably because I didn't want to be noticed—as if by my not seeing I couldn't be seen) and shot to my feet.

I was already born again, but as he spoke, I was overcome with the longing that if my heart could possibly hold more of God I wanted it. I wanted more, more, more of God. I didn't know what more of God meant, but I wanted more! I would have scraped out my insides if it would make more room for Him. As I was repeating the prayer, I realized that I wasn't speaking English. I wasn't speaking any language I knew, but the language was flowing, flowing, flowing out of my mouth.

I was loudly, fluently, speaking a language I'd never heard. As I prayed in this tongue, I started to weep. Changes. First, Neil coming in as a believer in Jesus, and now this infilling of the Holy Spirit so that I was infused with a boldness to proclaim Jesus. And this boldness has never left me. What a change from the meek young woman in the teachers' lunchroom who was too intimidated to admit she knew Jesus!

 Footprints 

"But you will receive power when the Holy Spirit comes upon you. And you will be my witnesses, telling people about me everywhere—in Jerusalem, throughout Judea, in Samaria, and to the ends of the earth (Acts 1:8 NLT).

Oh! I was filled with such a power, such boldness! It was there 24/7. Boldness!

I knew I didn't want Neil to flounder like I had, so I needed to find another Jewish person who was in love with Jesus. Who? Where would I find him or her? A third change! Not only was I loving Jesus and learning about Him, but I was also reaching out to bring others in. I was the disciple who was beginning to disciple others. Who would know any Jews who knew Jesus?

I loved my girls' pediatrician. Dr. Wimmer was relaxed and casual about health. Maybe raising eight children of his own had made him realize that most emergencies work themselves out if left be. On the visit after Jesus had come into my car, I told him every detail, and he told me that he was a Spirit-filled Catholic. I had not been sure at that time what Spirit-filled meant, but he loved the Lord and prayed. In fact, when I told him that Erica had unequal pupils with one considerably larger than the other, I suggested that we pray, and we did. I prayed with him in agreement, and her pupils immediately evened out. Later, when she developed a large knot on her forehead, I took her in to his office again.

"Cheryl, you prayed before. Let's do it again." We did and the knot left.

So now, I had the problem of Neil, the Jewish man who now loved Jesus. Was there a place for him? Was there anyone who would know what to do with him, with us?

Dr. Wimmer told me about a man who owned a carpet business. "Al Warner owns a carpet business, but carpets don't come first to Al. Jesus does. No one gets down to carpets before they get down to Jesus in Al's store. He has a prayer room in the back of the shop. Give him a call."

I called him. I started briefly to tell him about Neil, but then I heard Neil's car drive up. I had to hang up because, by this time, Al was talking animatedly and loudly, with so much zeal, that I thought he would be too much for Neil. So, I thanked Mr. Warner and hung up.

But Dr. Wimmer had given me another name, a chiropractor named Dr. Jeffrey Citrin.

So, the following morning I called the number. "Hello, is this the Citrin residence?"

"Yes, this is Candy."

"Candy, Neil and I are Jewish. My husband was just born again. I want him to be with other Jewish people who love Jesus. Are you Jewish?"

"No, but Jeff is."

"Candy, can we please come over some evening?"

She hesitated just a little. "Sure."

I pressed, "Can we come tonight?"

Another pause. "Yes, come on over tonight. I'll call Jeff and let him know."

Neil walked in the door and when I told him we were to be at Citrins at 7:00, he agreed.

We arrived at Jeff and Candy Citrin's modest home on Villa Maria in Hazelwood, and they welcomed us. Neil told them his story.

Footprints

Modest home. Yes they had a modest home, but God has so blessed them because they were incredibly generous with us, with their substance, time, and love.

"Give, and it will be given to you; a good measure—pressed down, shaken together, and running over—will be poured into your lap. For with the measure you use, it will be measured back to you" (Luke 6:38 HCSB).

"Well, you can go to church with us."

"No way!" Neil said. "This is enough. I'm going to be a closet Christian. I will never step foot in a church."

"You can't do that," said Jeff emphatically. "You must declare His name. You must learn. You must be with other believers."

"I have Laverne Anderson. She's all I need. Churches give me the creeps," said Neil. "People who said they were Christians murdered the Jews."

"So, don't worry," Jeff said peaceably. "This isn't a church. It's a grocery store."

"A grocery store? Well, I refuse to wear a tie."

"No one wears ties. Wear jeans. Just come."

"Oh. And do you want to receive the baptism of the Holy Spirit with the evidence of prayimg in tongues?" Jeff asked.

Neil shrugged. "Might as well. I've gone this far."

So they went into the kitchen, and Neil received the fullness of the Holy Spirit and prayer language.

Footprints

And they were all filled with the Holy Ghost, and began to speak with other tongues, as the Spirit gave them utterance (Acts 2:4 KJV).

I am not saying this happens to everyone. I am only recounting what happened to Neil and me.

The following Tuesday evening, Neil and I walked into a building and looked for Jeff and Candy who were sitting on the front row. Jeff was right. It was a grocery store that had been converted into a gathering place for lots of people who were dancing and singing with their hands in the air. It was really odd, but a great odd. I couldn't imagine what Neil was thinking. As we made our way up front, the music started.

Verses of the song, "Lion of Judah on the Throne," were on a screen. Musicians and rapturous congregants were singing as if directly to God, as if they could see Him. Even before we took our places, Neil was singing gustily with both hands in the air, praying in tongues.

It was as if part two of our lives had begun.

Meet the Author

Cheryl Samelson Skid was born in Michigan City, Indiana, and spent the first 17 years of her life in the love and protection of the Jewish community. Indiana University opened the doors to wild living after years of being protected as a daughter beloved by her parents. Between her sophomore and junior years of college, an opportunity opened to live as a volunteer in Israel, and she took it. Everything changed. The foolish coed gave way to the young woman who helped frightened North African and Middle Eastern immigrants prepare for war.

Cheryl has been married forty-three years to Neil, was a stay-at-home mom in Florissant, Missouri, until her last child was in kindergarten, and afterward spent twenty-five years teaching English and French, special education, and Bible. She still loves teaching and, as a retired educator, finds many opportunities to share her knowledge.

Cheryl with her Great Pyrenees, Avalanche

Her love of writing began when she was a child. Once she had her miraculous encounter with Jesus, she began keeping journals, recording thirty-eight years of God's amazing grace and power, which provided great material for her books. Her first book, *Taking God's Word to Heart*, is a 31-day devotional journal. *Never Out of His Sight* is her second book. Follow Cheryl on Facebook (Facebook.com/Chery.Skid) or visit her website (www.cherylskid.com).

Order Info

For autographed copies
or to schedule speaking engagements, contact:

Cheryl Skid
Women with a Vision
P. O. Box 693
Florissant, MO 63032 USA
(314) 603-5687
cherylskid@gmail.com

$16.95 plus $7 S/H

For bulk order discounts, contact the publisher.

Fruitbearer Publishing, LLC
P. O. Box 777, Georgetown, DE 19947
(302) 856-6649 • FAX (302) 856-7742
info@fruitbearer.com
www.fruitbearer.com

Made in the USA
San Bernardino, CA
27 May 2016